Advance Praise

"Jeffrey C. Goldfarb's life is a testimony to the value of relentless deep thinking about what it means to constitute an ethical and just social life across tremendous divides. In *Gray is Beautiful*, he thinks together with Hannah Arendt and Alexis de Tocqueville, with Adam Michnik and Václav Havel, with his students in New York and young people studying surreptitiously in Taliban-controlled Afghanistan, with former dissidents in Eastern Europe and Palestinian and Israeli peace activists. Sometimes, he concludes, uncertainty is productive, ambiguity essential, and anti-utopianism morally imperative. With absolute sobriety he sees the pluralism of values: sometimes some good things can be in tension with one another. While not optimistic, the author is incorrigibly hopeful, *contra spem spero*, and his determination to overcome cynicism is an inspiration to all of us."

Marci Shore, Chair in European Intellectual History,
Munk School of Global Affairs and Public Policy,
University of Toronto, Canada

"It is easy to think that dark times, like ours, demand the bright lights of grand theory, but in *Gray is Beautiful* Jeffrey C. Goldfarb offers us what we truly need: not perfect solutions, but the steady effort to illuminate the dilemmas of our day—dilemmas that we cannot eliminate but instead must work through together. With accessible prose and the kind of deep insight into our political and social life that arises only from a lifetime of scholarship, Goldfarb here calls for the formation of a radical center capable of resisting those who would snuff out the light generated by free public life. In so doing, this book holds important lessons for all who are concerned for the future of democracy, but particularly for those who, like me, need to be reminded of the value of committing ourselves not to the perfect, but to the better."

Fr. Patrick Gilger, SJ
Director, McNamara Center for the Study of Religion,
Loyola University, Chicago, USA

"This book makes a case for the radical centre as an ethical approach to the large questions that face society. Goldfarb argues that the centre need not be 'moderate' or conservative, but rather that it is a space in which judgements can be made from the recognition of social complexity and uncertainty.

The book takes theoretical inspiration from Hannah Arendt on the crucial distinction between fact and truth, and from the ethical and political stances of key actors in the transition from communism in eastern Europe. These engagements suggest to Goldfarb that even in (or is it especially in?) repressive societies, it is the grey zone of social interactions that offers the possibility of democracy—understood in this book as a package of elements including liberal rights and to a lesser extent social rights.

Goldfarb's personal experiences of working in different contexts add considerable heft and authenticity to his arguments. His accounts are at times moving, always thought-provoking. The writing is engaging, and the broad sweep of late twentieth-century/twenty-first-century events provides a compelling hook for his theoretical arguments."

Shireen Hassim, Canada150 Research Chair in Gender
and African Politics, Carleton University, Canada

"Gray Is Beautiful: Confronting the Retreat of Democracy from the Radical Center is a terrific book. For many decades, Jeff Goldfarb, the author of numerous books and innumerable essays, has been one of our major practitioners of a genuinely public sociology. As the creator of Public Seminar and the convenor of Democracy Seminar, he has been at the center of a global network of academics dedicated to promoting democracy through a 'politics of small things.' In this book, he reflects on some of the most difficult challenges of our time, from the ethics of collaboration to the practice of freedom in the face of authoritarianism. Written in the spirit of Hannah Arendt, each chapter presents a rich and engaging 'thought train,' inviting readers to join Goldfarb in the process of 'thinking what we are doing.' The book both confronts the retreat of democracy and contributes towards its revitalization."

Jeffrey C. Isaac, James H. Rudy Professor of Political Science at Indiana University, Bloomington

"Gray is Beautiful is an invaluable guide for thinking about the retreat of democracy and polarization of politics in our time. In response to political platforms fueled by algorithms, echo chambers, and conspiracy theories, Jeffrey C. Goldfarb calls for the revitalization of free public spaces that embrace shades of gray over the polar opposition of black and white. The ideological dogmatism of left and right, he persuasively argues, can be overcome by embracing a radical center that is open and inclusive.

Drawing on Hannah Arendt, Adam Michnik, Václav Havel, Erving Goffman, and Alexis de Tocqueville, Goldfarb seeks alternatives to the transactional cynicism of our times and incremental politics of accommodation to political extremism. Responding to the rapid dismantling of democratic institutions, erosion of civility, and pervasive cynicism and post-truth denial of facts, Goldfarb concludes his inquiry with cogent critique of what he calls 'neo-totalitarianism.'

Resistance to neo-totalitarian attacks on migrants, universities, the rule of law and free speech entails the renewal of free public spaces. The way forward, Goldfarb maintains, is to accept the uncertainties of our social condition while simultaneously seeking alternatives with one another. Hope for the future of democratic inclusion and civility is rooted in the politics of small things and transformative power of artistic expression. In the spirit of Hannah Arendt, *Gray is Beautiful* calls for a renewed commitment to dialogue, the openness of public spaces, freedom of artistic expression, and the power of the radical center."

Siobhan Kattago, Associate Professor of Philosophy,
University of Tartu, Estonia

GRAY IS BEAUTIFUL

CEU PRESS
PERSPECTIVES

How did we get to the precarious state that we find ourselves in today? What new thinking is needed to tackle the big problems we face? Offering the latest perspectives on both new and perennial issues, books in this series address a wide range of topics of critical importance. An international collection of leading authors encourages us to look at topics from different viewpoints; to think outside the box. Launched to commemorate 30 years of the CEU Press, the series looks to stimulate debates on the broader issues of the day.

Published in the series:

» Ranabir Samaddar, *Biopolitics from Below: Crisis, Conjuncture, Rupture*

» Matt Qvortrup, *The Political Brain: The Emergence of Neuropolitics*

» Per Högselius and Achim Klüppelberg, *The Soviet Nuclear Archipelago: A Historical Geography of Atomic-Powered Communism*

» Éric Fassin, *State Anti-Intellectualism and the Politics of Gender and Race*

GRAY IS BEAUTIFUL

Confronting the Retreat of Democracy
from the Radical Center

Jeffrey C. Goldfarb

CEU PRESS

ISBN 978 96 3386 861 4
e-ISBN 978 96 3386 862 1 (pdf)
e-ISBN 9789 63 386 863 8 (accessible ePub)
DOI 10.5117/9789633868614
NUR 697

Cover design and layout: Éva Szalay

For Ludo, Benji, and Levi

Table of Contents

Preface and Acknowledgements

"The retreat of democracy," worldwide has been progressing rapidly as I have been writing this book, especially in the United States. Donald Trump's unprecedented attacks on democracy have escalated. The examples cited in the book have been followed by even more radical attacks. And the blend of cynical absolutism and dogmatic true belief, with cynicism feeding dogmatism, and dogmatism feeding cynicism, has advanced evermore strongly. This confirms my concluding contention that we are experiencing the rise of a distinctive form of totalitarian culture, *neo-totalitarianism*.

And as I have been writing and attempting to properly address the unfolding tragedies of the Israeli-Palestinian conflict, its atrocities and war crimes also have escalated. I was reluctant to use the word *genocide* to describe the Israeli campaign in Gaza, concerned as I am that the conflict should not be understood as a clear black and white matter. But as this book goes to press, I am now convinced that it is the proper word to describe the killing and harming of tens of thousands of Palestinians, the imposition of a near total siege, including blocking humanitarian aid, leading to mass starvation; systematically destroying the healthcare and education systems in Gaza, and carrying out systematic and widespread attacks on religious and cultural sites. While this has not been a repetition of the Holocaust in Europe, leading to my reticence to use the word, genocide, the internationally accepted legal definition of the term as it has been applied in the recent past to the atrocities against the Tutsi in Rwanda, the Bosnia Muslims in Bosnia and Herzegovina, and the Rohingya in Myanmar, I am convinced, applies as well to the atrocities against Palestinians in Gaza.[1]

While *neo-totalitarianism* and *genocide* reveal the darkness of our times, they also suggest to me the pressing significance of "the gray is beautiful" political aesthetic and the radical centrist political commitment that I have explored from different angles, drawing upon various experiences and analyses, in the chapters that follow. I hope, in the not-too-distant future, a new edition of this book will be required to demonstrate the cogency of my arguments as people confront the retreat of democracy with wisdom and significant consequences.

Any changes I would make would be informed by and primarily directed to the communities of teachers, colleagues, students, and readers I have worked with and addressed while writing this book, and in my earlier writing, research, teaching, and academic and civic engagements. With this in mind, I wish to thank for their support over the years my teachers, colleagues, and students at the State University of New York at Albany, the University of Chicago, the American University of Afghanistan, and the New School for Social Research, my primary intellectual home for almost fifty years. I also gratefully acknowledge the direct and indirect financial support of the International Research and Exchanges Board, the Ford Foundation, the Open Society Foundation, and the Carnegie Corporation of New York, as well as Michael E. Gellert, a major donor to The New School and a significant supporter of my work in East Central Europe and New York.

I have a sense that I am part of a transnational community of intellectuals and citizens, at universities and beyond, that has struggled for democratic decency. We have worked together and experienced the highs and lows of the recent past. We have been part of movements that have yielded wonderful results, an improvement of civil rights in the U.S., the expansion of gender, sexual, racial and economics rights and justice worldwide, the democratic wave at the end of the twentieth century in Southern Europe and in East and Central Europe, and Central and South America, as well as Asia, and Africa. We have also faced defeats, from the failures of the Arab Uprisings to the backsliding of the democratic resurgence in East Central Europe, to the global retreat of democracy that we are now experiencing. During these ups and downs, I have benefitted from the advice and criticism of many colleagues. They are too numerous to name individually here, but I trust they know who they are.

There are a few, though, I must mention, people with whom I have had significant discussions as I have been writing this book about the beauty of the gray, the radical, central importance of a free public life, and the retreat of democracy: Talal Asad, Muska Dastageer, Daniel Dayan, Irit Dekel, Nancy Hanrahan, Jeffrey C. Isaac, Elżbieta Matynia, William Milberg, Haroun Rahimi, and Michael Weinman. I have especially benefitted from Hanrahan's close reading of earlier drafts of the manuscript for which I am deeply grateful. When I sat at my desk and tried to understand the world I have experienced, I have had a sense that I have not been alone, but instead felt that I have been continuing my in-depth conversations with these thinking comrades, these friends.

I also imagine that I have been talking with my students, who have taught me so much over the years about what is coming next. Most recently, these students have included those in my classes at the American University of Afghanistan. Their commitment to learning and their intellectual seriousness, despite all the obstacles they face, has inspired me.

Much closer to home, I have been inspired by the young people in my family, my grandsons, Ludovic Gouéry, Benjamin Goldfarb, and Levi Goldfarb, to whom I dedicate this book. Their intelligence, creativity, and energy provide hope against my feeling of despair that it has come to this.

1. The Sensibility, the Commitment, the Context, and the Approach

The Sensibility

Ever since hearing a moving lecture, "Gray is Beautiful" by Adam Michnik, at the New School for Social Research in November of 1996, I've been circling around a sensibility and its significance, critically analyzing the limitations of the black and white solutions, exploring the promise of the gray. For over twenty-five years, I've been developing this book.

Gray Is beautiful: In this paradoxical assertion, Michnik, one of the most important democratic intellectuals of East Central Europe, reflected upon the similarities and the differences between the youthful protests on both sides of the Iron Curtain. On the one hand, "'The world as it is' meant an unjust world." On the other, there were young people who aspired to live in that very world. "(T)he students of Berkeley and Paris rejected the order of bourgeois democracy, as the students of Prague and Warsaw were fighting for the freedom bourgeois democracy guaranteed."[2]

These words spoke to me because I had been both active in the student movement that started in Berkeley and active as a young researcher in Warsaw. And during my years working in Warsaw, in the movement for democracy in East Central Europe, I spent a good deal of time collaborating with Michnik and many of his friends and colleagues.

In his lecture, he explained why they, in the democratic opposition in Poland, Czechoslovakia, Hungary, and beyond, opposed Communism: "it was a lie, and we were searching for the truth." But he also explained how the certainties of those times that brought socialists, conservatives, nationalists, and religious critics together in the opposition posed dangers after the Communists left the political stage. This is the danger of absolutism, of blind certainty, of excessive political clarity.

> The heroism of the people who resisted repression has shown its second face: intolerant, fanatical, and opposed to new modernizing ideas. This is a natural turn of events in post-communist democracies.[3]

Thus, he called, and I have seconded the call, for a "gray democracy," animated by competing ideals and utopian visions, but not overwhelmed by the visions to the point that "all sides become incapable of compromise." Michnik continued:

> Democracy is a continuous articulation of particular interests, a diligent search for compromise among them, a marketplace of passions, emotions, hatreds, and hopes; it is eternal imperfection, a mixture of sinfulness, saintliness, and monkey business.[4]

This rings true to me. While Michnik focused on his experience in Poland and around the old Soviet bloc, I have been exploring broader implications far beyond that region. Inspired by his essay, I've published a series of pieces in *Public Seminar* and on the platform of *Democracy Seminar*,[5] commenting on the politics of the day and enduring political problems from a gray perspective. While he considered the transition from Communism and anti-Communism to post-Communism, I have been considering present challenges facing democracy in both long-established liberal democracies, such as those in North America and Western Europe, and in polities with little, or practically no democratic experience, such as the polities of East and Central Europe, but also of those of Latin America, Africa, and Asia. In recent years in Afghanistan, I have been working on these issues with students and colleagues at the American University of Afghanistan, a long way from Warsaw and Prague, and Paris and Berkeley.

The Commitment: The Radical Center

My research, writing, and teaching have taken me around the world, observing people confronting a diverse set of political problems and dilemmas. I've observed firsthand how people seek to overcome injustice and oppression. I have observed how black and white approaches to problems so often miss the mark, that things are more complex. I have drawn from this, inspired by Michnik, an appreciation of the beauty of the gray. Yet, I also realize that that's not enough, that there are different shades of gray, and that discerning the perfect shade is impossible. This is where free, open, public space is most relevant, where a democratic life resides. There must be a way that the less than perfect ways of proceeding can be opened up for discussion, considered, and judged.

Things do appear to be coming apart. Polarization and anomie have become two sides of the same distressing coin, wherever I look, near and far from my home in New York. Political opinions abound. People are struggling to make sense of the world, while a shared common sense, even a shared factual truth, is elusive. I see a need for a primary commitment to public interaction and deliberation, a commitment to work to address fundamental problems, among people of diverse opinions and judgments. There is a need for a radical commitment to a free public domain. In this sense, I am a radical centrist.

Here some glimpses of this commitment:

Israel/Gaza: As I am writing this introduction, the war continues, thousands are being killed. The whole world has been watching. The October 7, 2023, Hamas attack on Israeli civilians was atrocious: They murdered over 1,200 people, took about 250 hostage, committed rape, massacred revelers at a music festival, and terrorized men, women and children in their homes. In my judgment, the attack must be condemned in no uncertain terms, no matter where you stand on the intractable Israeli-Palestinian conflict.

Likewise, the Israeli response in subsequent weeks and months has been atrocious: over sixty-seven thousand killed, the population dislocated, homes, neighborhoods, entire cities and towns decimated, food and medical care in desperate short supply, widespread hunger, and disease. As soon as the dimensions and cruelty of the Hamas attack were clear, I anticipated and feared such an Israeli response. Now, I think it should forthrightly be condemned, again, independent of where one stands on the conflict between Israelis and Palestinians.

Yet, sadly, and predictably, what I think should happen, universal condemnation of atrocities and war crimes, has not taken place. People on both sides have disappointed me. Too many of my friends, colleagues, and students on the left in New York and beyond, judged the Hamas attack positively or at least rationalized it as a necessary response to settler colonialism in which all Israelis, the elderly, the young, and the infirm, along with soldiers, are enemy combatants. And among too many of my Jewish friends, community members, and family, there has been a parallel lack of concern about the humanity and suffering of Gazans. No distinction is made between Hamas militants and civilians. They must be vanquished. They are all enemies of the Jewish state, antisemites.

In and beyond Israel and Palestine, there has been a tendency to choose sides, and the self-proclaimed radicals, those who seek to get to the root of the problem, are purportedly those who clearly decide which side they are on. Radical pro-Zionists know the imperative of the Jewish homeland, of the Jewish state, as the answer to the ubiquitous scourge of antisemitism. Radical pro-Palestinians know that the Jewish Israelis are settler colonialists, who don't belong on the land of Palestine. The problem for Zionists is eternal antisemitism, and therefore the just creation of a Jewish state, in the Jewish biblical homeland, was a necessity, as is its defense, whatever the human costs. The root of the problem for radical Palestinians is the invasion of foreign colonists who have disregarded the humanity of the Indigenous people. They must go back to where they came from. "Palestine will be free, from the river to the sea."

Such radicals ignore the tragic dimension of the ongoing conflict, on the small piece of land of Israel-Palestine. Both Jewish Israelis and Palestinian Arabs have reasons to be there. Neither is going to disappear. They will live together or die together. Between the political and religious justifications for exclusive rights of either side, the central imperative is that they recognize, confront each other and their competing positions, and seek to accommodate each other. How they accomplish this, if they accomplish this, is uncertain. A two-state solution? A one-state solution? Some form of federation or confederation?

The position "between" is the truly radical one that recognizes the fundamental facts on the ground and seeks a just resolution of the conflict, with strong commitment to conflicting interests.[6] It is far from certain how this ground in between the conflicting parties and those individuals committed to these parties can be constituted. This is extremely difficult given the structured military and political inequality that exists between the conflicting parties. There are, nonetheless, peace groups committed to this position that consciously work through the difficulties this presents. Political leaders have the capacity to create such space. However, such groups and leaders have come up short. It is within the creative culture of the radical center in architecture, art, poetry, literature, theater, music, and film that we can see zones of interaction and deliberation opening up. I will explore this power of creative culture as we proceed.

Capitalism versus Socialism: The struggle of the Cold War was between the so-called free world and the Communist totalitarian one. Or seen from the other side, it was a struggle between the progressive socialist democratic forces and capitalism, with all its negative consequences, including colonialism, racism, and class exploitation. Stripped of such charged imagery, there was a fundamental conflict between those who were committed to socialism as the systemic answer to the injustices of capitalism, and those who understood the close connection between free markets, political freedom, and individual freedom. There were radical positions. Among those who supported "democratic capitalism" some maintained that the free market was *the* key to individual freedom and democracy. And among those who supported socialism, there were those who thought that all that stood between the liberation of humanity, and its prolonged suffering, was the control of "the mode of production," with such intellectuals as Hayek and Friedman on one side, and Marx and a wide array of Marxists on the other. And among those of the less radical bent, there were ideas about "a third way." They would moderately take a bit of capitalism and add a bit of socialism and propose one formula or another, one third way or another.

While I appreciate the critical insights of theorists and scholars on both sides of this divide, and I admit that I have found aspects of third ways appealing, I think they all mislead when they directly apply theory to practice, advocating theoretical solutions to political problems: true socialism, capitalism, or a third way.

At this point, I want to make something clear: my commitment to the center is not necessarily a commitment to a middle ground or a moderate path. Rather it is a commitment to centering different, even conflicting, insights and principles, a commitment to dialogue, to democratic deliberation addressing crucial questions, a commitment to a free, open, democratic public.

The Context: The Retreat of Democracy

I fear that such a commitment is waning, that wherever we look, we observe new autocratic leaders attacking democracy, with a weak or disorganized defense of democracy. Among the autocrats in power: Bukele in El Salvador, Erdogan in Turkey, Fico in Slovakia, Netanyahu in Israel, Orban in Hungary, Milei in Argentina, Modi in India, Meloni in Italy, Putin in Russia, and Trump in the United States, or the would-be autocrats out of power, but threatening: Abascal in Spain, Bolsonaro in Brazil, Farage in the United Kingdom, Kaczynski in Poland, Le Pen in France, Wilders in the Netherlands, among others. These leaders have significant popular support. They have won popular majorities, usually with a combination of enthusiastic supporters and those who support them for one limited reason or another, responding to unpopular liberal or leftist rule, though there is a similar type of left-wing autocrat, as well, who gain power with a similar kind of support, such as Ortega in Nicaragua and Maduro in Venezuela.

As broad social developments have led to the ascendance of these autocrats, they threaten to transform political and cultural life. People are seeking easy answers to perplexing problems, with the autocrats presenting easy solutions. They tell their constituents who is to blame, and they present themselves as the solution to the problems. They are the answers to the problems of globalization, mass migrations, unjust inequalities, changes in gender and race relations, foreigners, unemployment, inflation, natural and not-so-natural disasters.

The United States is at the forefront of this development, with his fellow autocrats following President Trump's lead. This is shocking to Americans, as well as to those beyond our borders. It's not that demagoguery, xenophobia, racism, misogyny, political persecution, and repression are unknown in American history, far from it. But that this seamy side of democracy, anticipated by Alexis de Tocqueville, as we will consider in chapter 7, is now centered in the White House and is inspiring autocrats worldwide is unprecedented.

My work trying to understand how democratic activists have resisted repression in the totalitarian contexts now has direct application to such a broad range of countries around the world, including first and foremost, the United States. I have experience working in totalitarian contexts, for many years in East Central Europe, especially in Poland, and in Central Asia, specifically in Afghanistan. In chapter 3, I present my reflections on the significance of my experiences, as a student, scholar, researcher, and citizen of the United States, seeking to understand my country, appreciating its democratic promise, as well as the practices that have not lived up to that promise. I never anticipated that my work in repressive societies would have such direct application to the United States as it does now.

In the chapters that follow, I will consider the present repressive context in a deliberate fashion. We will open with a series of inquiries that illuminate what I take to be the wise political action within the ever more apparent retreat of democracy. We will explore the beauty of the gray and the commitment to the radical center, considering the promise of uncertainty (chapter 2), the role of the democratic intellectual (chapter 3), the nature of the radical center through an analysis of the political thinking of Hannah Arendt (chapter 4), and art as a way of appreciating the beauty of the gray and cultivating free, critical dialogues about pressing social issues (chapter 5). We will then turn to an examination of the possibilities of public action within the most extreme of circumstances, in Afghanistan (chapters 6) and within the American context, using Alexis de Tocqueville to understand the retreat of democracy in America and to understand ways of responding to the retreat (chapter 7). This will lead us to confront a major question of our times "to collaborate or not to collaborate," with whom and against whom in the present political context (chapter 8).

In the concluding chapters, I will qualify my fundamental thesis: that gray is preferrable to black and white, holding promise for better social arrangements, even if not the best. In the earlier chapters, I will have explored gray zones. I will have considered the wisdom of committing to the better over waiting for or insisting upon the best. I will have focused on uncertainty, dilemma, ambiguity, ambivalence, and unanticipated consequence. Yet, there is also a need to be clear and certain on some issues, when it is a matter of the black and the white. I will show how this is the case in our present context. In chapters 9 and 10, I will show how our present circumstance is characterized by a distinctive form of cynical rule, with a family resemblance to the totalitarianism of the twentieth century. I will show how the commitment to the radical center and the appreciation of the political beauty of the gray is a strategic way of opposing the present repressive threat, as it was a highly effective way of opposing twentieth-century totalitarianism.

Approach: The Social Condition

Before we proceed, I would like to clarify the theoretical approach that underpins this inquiry. I want to make clear that the gray is beautiful aesthetic and the radical commitment to the center are predicated upon a sociological understanding that runs counter to the prevailing approaches to social and political inquiry. Generally, social scientists seek to provide explanations and accounts of how the social world works with priority given to causal analysis, seeking to explain how a set of social phenomena explain specified results. In the radical version of this, the goal is to "predict and control." There is great debate about which set explains what results. For example, do material conditions or cultural ones account for the persistence of racial inequality in American life, or the persistence of economic inequality, or the formation of one sort of political regime or another? Problems are identified, explanations are researched, and solutions are proposed. Much is learned in this process. But there are dangers. There is a tendency to confuse hypothetical scientific solutions, which are confirmed or disconfirmed through research, with political ones. The social world, in its rich complexity, is oversimplified, even when there is recognition of complex probabilities, when, for example, it is recognized that both material and cultural explanations must be taken into account.

This has led me, along with several colleagues and students, to consider a different approach, an approach that starts with an understanding of limitation and sees this understanding as an intriguing opening for democracy, for public deliberation, for individual and collective agency.

The task is to identify and examine the tensions that are inevitably built into the social fabric and explore the ways people work to address the dilemmas the tensions pose.

Some examples:

It is important for a democratic society to provide equal opportunity for all young people. The less privileged should have the advantages of a good education. This is certainly a most fundamental requirement for equal opportunity. On the other hand, it is just as certain that a good society, democratic and otherwise, should encourage and enable parents to provide the best for their children, to read to them, to introduce them to the world of human creativity, and to provide them with interesting experiences, both near and far. But not all parents can do this effectively: some have the means, some don't. Democratic education and caring for one's children are in tension. The social bonds of citizenship and the social bonds of family are necessarily at odds. This tension, in many variations, defines a significant dimension of the social condition. The tension yields dilemmas for practical action. The task for research is to illuminate the tensions and the dilemmas and to study how the dilemmas have been addressed, for better and for worse. The hope is that such research can inform debate about future courses of action, with an understanding that there are no perfect solutions, but only gray ones, and that the only way to get to the most workable gray solution is through public deliberation, a primary political commitment, the commitment to a radical center.

Another dimension of the social condition was illuminated in a classic lecture, "Politics as a Vocation," by Max Weber: the tension between what he called "the ethics of responsibility" versus "the ethics of ultimate ends." I observed an iteration of this tension in the debate about *Lincoln*, the movie. In politics, there is always a tension between getting things done, as Weber would put it, "responsibly," and being true to one's principles. Ideally the tension is in balance, as it was portrayed in the film: Lincoln, the realist, enabled Thaddeus Stevens, the idealist, to realize his ends in less than ideal ways. A wise politician, Weber maintained, and the movie explored, knows how to balance idealism with realism.

And this tension goes beyond individual judgment and political effectiveness. Establishing the social support to realize ideals is necessary, but sometimes the creation of such supports makes it next to impossible for the ideals to be realized. Making sure that educational ideals are realized, for example, equal opportunity, requires measurement of educational achievement, but the act of measurement can get in the way of real education. (Think about preparation for exams of entrance, such as the SATs in the United States, into much-sought-after educational institutions.) Making sure that funds distributed by an NGO do get to disaster victims can get in the way of getting the funds to the victims. Most generally, organizing to achieve some end establishes the conditions for those who have their particular interests in the organization itself to pursue their interests. NGOs often provide for a comfortable standard of living for their employees in impoverished parts of the world, sometimes this gets in the way of realizing organizational ends. But this is not a new development, Robert Michels described this in the early twentieth century as "the iron law of oligarchy." I suggest that we think of this as a dilemma built into the social order of things.

I think, further, that one of the most fundamental manifestations of the social condition animates the work of Erving Goffman. He explored the power of the Thomas theorem (the political implications of which we will consider in chapter 6), more intensely than any other social theorist. *If people in a situation define something as real, it is real in its consequences.* Goffman was particularly interested in how in their expressive behavior people managed to define social reality.

The dilemma arises when people disagree about the reality, are ambivalent about it, or even want to flee from it. The prime example is the concept and apparent reality of race. It's a social construction, as every American college freshman comes to know. It's a fiction, but a fiction that we cannot ignore, a fiction that we continue to treat as real, and in doing so becomes a social fact. To pretend that it doesn't matter is to flee from enduring social problems. But attending to the problem of race carefully has unintended consequence, furthering its continued salience in social life. Recognize race, and it continues to be real. Ignore race, and it's likely that you will ignore its continued negative effects. Controversies over "Diversity, Equity, and Inclusion" (DEI) initiatives revolve around this dilemma of race. Those who maintain that administrative DEI projects solve the problem of racism overlook this dilemma. They propose easy solutions, a variety of administrative actions and exercises, to a complex problem. Those who attack them and overlook the dilemma in an opposing way, ignoring the continuing power of race, though, have made matters worse, as we will explore in the conclusion of our inquiry.

I worry when social observers and political actors pretend that the complications of the social condition can be easily overcome, following one formula or another, with negative political consequences. Realizing that this is not possible, leads me to the gray political aesthetic and to the commitment to the radical center.

In the following chapters, I will explore the relationships between this analysis, political commitment, and aesthetic. Versions of most of the chapters were originally presented as public talks, which were purposely constructed to provoke discussion. In the chapters that were not previously publicly presented, the same dialogic form will be used. I will imagine giving new talks to an imagined audience, the readers of this book.

2. Uncertainty in Times of Pandemic: Confronting the Social Condition

On September 12, 2021, I delivered the keynote lecture at the Graduate School for Social Research Summer School, in Wierzba, Poland. I was asked to give a talk about uncertainty, and I used the occasion to reflect upon its promise, not primarily its most obvious perils.

Here, I open our exploration of the beauty of the gray with a revised version of that lecture. I seek to demonstrate that the conditions of our uncertainty can be illuminated and understood, and that this is an opportunity for opening centered dialogue, for constituting free public interaction, for confronting the social condition.

God is not dead. The specter of Communism, the thousand-year Reich, and the end of history have all passed. Secularization and urbanization clearly have their limits, and capitalism and liberal democracy have waxed and waned. Our certainties about long term, inevitable, and permanent transformations, based on science and pseudo-science, have collapsed, again and again. The grand historical narratives and grand macro-comparative historical, social scientific theories have misled, in my judgment, more often than they have illuminated.

I note this as uncertainty overwhelms us today, without the assurances provided by modernization theories of one sort or another, be they Marxist or Weberian, Parsonian or neo-Marxist, or neo-Weberian. The uncertainty is overwhelming, even revealed in the way I am joining you today.

I accepted the invitation to join this summer school, fully intending to deliver this lecture in person, and to talk with you about your work. But the Delta variant of COVID-19 got in the way. I thought the vaccine and public health measures would ensure that I could return to the normal, but I was wrong. Did I make the right decision in not joining you in person? I am far from certain.

I also had plans to give lectures in Lithuania and Hungary. The itinerary was like one I had as the pandemic exploded in March of 2020 to meet colleagues working on *Democracy Seminar*, a worldwide committee of democratic correspondence that I chair.[7] Then, as now, I felt it would be wise to stay closer to home. Then, my decision was questioned by some of my colleagues. I remember vividly that one in Budapest objected, pointing out that there were only a handful of cases in the first week of the month. But by the end of the month, I very well may have been stranded, as the world locked down, likely I would have been in Budapest. I don't expect the same thing to happen, but exactly what will happen is not clear at all, and I think we should note that this is more a consequence of sociological factors than virological ones.

In the past year and a half, we have observed good science and public health practices outfox the virus, but we have also observed the virus fighting back. In this battle, there have been sound responses and crazy ones.

I think it is clear, we can get through this sooner rather than later with wise public decisions by officials and citizens. But we can't count on such wisdom, with some authoritarian and demagogic leaders using pandemic lockdowns to tighten their controls and other such leaders, along with normal narrow-minded politicians, stigmatizing and politicizing science to enhance their power, often based on wild conspiracy theories. This has led to widespread refusals to vaccinate, mask, and social distance. The virus has been politicized. People are lining up for and against the vaccine, for and against vaccine passports, for and against masking, for and against social distancing.

This is madness, and it is unknown how decisive it will be. In much of the world, the virus devastates because of vaccine scarcity, but it is still devastating your part of the world, and, even more so in mine, in the United States, because of social, political, and cultural willful ignorance. How long the ignorance will prevail is unknown, though it is clear it has had a great immediate impact on the economy and society, and long-term effects.

And it is not only viruses that develop in this uncertain way. Uncertainty appears to be definitive of our times. As someone who has made a career for himself exploring the grounds for hope, I find myself struggling against despair, much more than usual.

Environmental disaster is now our lived experience. I've been concerned about this for more than fifty years, since the first Earth Day on April 22, 1970. I vividly remember the date as I, a young new leftist, enjoyed the irony that it was the one hundredth anniversary of the birth of Vladimir Lenin, as I helped organize the event in my community. It's always amazed me that that irony has not been broadly noted. More seriously, also ignored, for far too long, was the impending ecological disaster looming on the horizon. And now it seems as if we have reached that horizon, as fires rage, floods inundate, hurricanes devastate, and air and sea temperatures and sea levels reach record highs.

Yet, major political leaders and parties, and their followers, deny these harsh realities, explain them away or fatalistically accept them as acts of God, and sometimes even explaining them as consequences of sexual immorality, gender ideology, and abortion.

A new dark age seems to be upon us, more likely than not. Although I can't say, as I did about the pandemic, that climate change is primarily a political problem. I think it is safe to say that the solution to the ecological crisis, if there is one, is political. It requires marshaling human capacity, technical, but particularly political, to recognize the full dimensions of the problem and then act to address them. Thus, I turn to political uncertainty.

For a long time, there has been a consensus that the long arch of history points to democracy, what Alexis de Tocqueville characterized as a providential force.[8] In the twentieth century, this providence came in different and competing varieties, from the constitutional liberal democracy, in the former "free world," to the people's democracies of the former socialist bloc. And then, after the fall of the Soviet Empire, many thought liberal, capitalist democracy was inevitable. Francis Fukuyama penned the title, article, and then the book that named this perspective, "the end of history," but it was in fact a conclusion suggested by a long line of social and political thought.

As an American sociologist trained at the tail end of the hegemony of the theory of Talcott Parsons, this was the prevailing view, made most explicit in his final book, *The System of Modern Society*. But the kind of evolutionary progressive position that Parsons developed, and that his radical critics shared along with him, is no longer. We know that liberal democracy is far from inevitable, and we know, as well, that socialism as the systemic alternative to capitalism also is not. Further, as we face environmental disaster and the pandemic, it is not at all sure that liberal democracy is up to the task of effectively addressing the crises of our times, nor is it clear, especially to those of us who have some experience in your part of the world, that socialism provides the simple solution to our problems. There in Poland, I think socialism requires a brief word, while democracy requires a more deliberate consideration.

I'm perpetually puzzled by the notion that capitalism is the cause of the major problems we now face. That it is the fundamental problem. I remember when I thought it was so, when during a student demonstration in the spring of 1970, I denounced an environmental studies professor, disrupting his class, for not recognizing that the answer to the problems of climate change was the destruction of capitalism. I remember foolishly shouting at him, half inspired by Karl Marx, half inspired by Emile Durkheim, that there are no piecemeal solutions.

But now I am pretty sure that piecemeal solutions are all there is, or more precisely direct solutions. The problems of global warming require targeted solutions to address the pressing problems. Develop ways to ween the most and the least developed economies off fossil fuels. Develop clean energy. Regulate carbon emissions. Share new technologies. Plan to mitigate the inevitable upcoming disasters: flooding, drought, hurricanes, fires, extreme heat. Support the poor regions of the world to avoid escalating humanitarian disasters. I see no reason to believe that there exists a systemic alternative to capitalism, called socialism, that will provide a singular solution to these problems. Indeed, the evidence is that all attempts to create a systemic alternative to capitalism, around the Soviet bloc and far beyond, in the Americas, Africa and Asia, as well as Europe, have been just as bad as, if not worse than capitalism, concerning the environment, and much else.

The notion of a knowable systemic solution is part of the problem, not the solution, whether it is called socialism or goes by another name. A utopian plan for the future that replaces all that is wrong with the world can be imagined but thinking with certainty that it will provide in practice *the* solution for all that ails us is likely to repeat many of the horrors of the twentieth century.

Liberal democracy is another matter. In 1989, I didn't think that it had become inevitable or that it was in some way the end of history. Existing democracies, I saw quite clearly, left a lot to be desired, and enacting desire would constitute a real and contentious history. Nonetheless, I was quite impressed by democracy's global appeal. I was pretty sure that the attraction of ideological alternatives, of the left and the right, to actual existing democracy were things of the past. I was mistaken. I was too sure. I should have been less certain. Uncertainty would have been wise.

Socialism has made a surprising comeback, as have, more perniciously, various forms of fundamentalism and populism. Okay, another word about socialism to be sure I am not misunderstood. It all depends on how the notion is defined. If socialism is understood as a complete systemic alternative to capitalism, its comeback would be unfortunate, to say the least. But it is another matter if socialism is understood as a political project to qualify and control the excesses of the market and the hegemony of private property, to ensure social and economic justice, and decency: a socialism of grays, not of blacks and whites. This is just what we need, in my political, but not scientific, judgment, but it is far from certain that it will happen. It requires insight, understanding, and informed action. In this way, I am a socialist.

It is also far from certain that the normative practices that define the liberal and the democratic in liberal democracy will flourish: the rule of law, representative democracy, multi-party elections, the peaceful transfer of power, minority rights, free association, and freedom of the press, and of universities and the arts and sciences. I make the list because I want to emphasize that I believe liberal democracy is not a system, with one model. What we call liberal democracy is not one thing, but a combination of correlated, normative elements and practices, never fully realized and differently enacted. The term "liberal democracy," is a shorthand for naming these elements and for justifying them. So, as I raise the issue of the future of liberal democracy and note that it is uncertain, I am indicating a concern about the future of specific principles and practices that can be empirically appraised. I reiterate to emphasize: the rule of law, free media, academic freedom, representative democracy, minority rights, and pluralism.[9]

These futures are, to be sure, connected, but they also have some relative independence and tensions. And these futures clearly are uncertain. To understand this, we should not formulate grand theories, but we should closely examine details and consider their broad significance.

Democracy, like God and the devil, is in the details. And when we examine the details, I think it becomes clear that there are ongoing contests, and the results are far from certain. And there is no inevitable historical or social structure which tells us how things will work out. It is all open to debate, leading to discussion, as we address numerous tensions and dilemmas.

Is there a future for democracy in America, Poland, and the rest of the world? When will the negative effects of the pandemic ever end? And even if they end in the foreseeable future, will the human species survive climate catastrophe?

Now, to my primary social scientific point: as unique as these questions seem to be, I would like to suggest that it may be wise for us to consider their normality, rather than their uniqueness, and then address them in these terms. Grand historical narratives and comparative historical narratives,

Marxist, anti-Marxist, and much in between, are predicated on causal chains. Committing to these narratives works against a sense of uncertainty, even as the narratives are tweaked to account for the unexpected.

The development of the mode of production and class relations move history from feudalism to capitalism, to socialism. The role of the Party is to move this development forward. As meaningful action is based more and more on rational orientation, the institutions of the economy and society are transformed, producing the modern world, with distinctive and relatively independent spheres of state, religion, culture as the arts and sciences, and form of authority, even a distinctive approach to sexuality. As solidarity is based more and more on difference and mutual interdependence, and not identity, a new type of society develops. Thus spoke, Karl Marx, Max Weber, and Emile Durkheim as they gave account of the development of the modern social order. But so much was not anticipated by these accounts: world wars, totalitarianism (which Hannah Arendt succinctly described as modern barbarism), religious revivals and fundamentalism, and the centrality of media in the constituting social order and social change.

With this in mind, I often imagine what would have happened if Gabriele Tarde won his debate with Durkheim over the primary subject matter of sociology, and how social science might have been better prepared to account for the experiences of the twentieth century and anticipate the problems of the twenty-first. What if what are often taken to be social structures would be understood as interactive patterns, that are sustained and are often quite durable, but also are changed dynamically through anticipated and unanticipated interactions? This imaginative experiment, I have come to realize, is similar to Bruno Latour's reimagination of sociology.

What if we recognized the uncertain consequences of social interaction as a core feature of social life as we experience it, their contingency, as Richard Rorty philosophically reflected on this? What if we recognized that the profound uncertainty we are now experiencing is characteristic of social life, and that the task of sociological, political, economic, and historical inquiry is not to maintain that these can be explained and resolved with set formulas and models, but seek instead to illuminate the uncertainties? I propose such a program, understanding that it has often been followed in practice, but has not been broadly recognized.

Social scientists have studied how the social order must be worked on to be sustained (think Harold Garfinkel), with a constant struggle of maintaining a working definition of the definition of social situation, with redefinition a persistent possibility. This has been classically examined in the sociology of Erving Goffman and the tradition of inquiry that preceded and followed him. The focus of such investigations has been on face-to-face interactions of a quotidian sort. But, as I have argued in *The Politics of Small Things*, big political and social topics can be illuminated using insights coming out of this theoretical tradition. Totalitarianism and its alternatives, and democracy and its enemies can be studied in this way, as can the other topics I am discussing here, the sociology of the environment and medical sociology.

What we do will determine whether COVID-19 will continue to fester and spread. It depends on what we do whether the modern economy, technology, instrumental rationality, and capitalism leads to human extinction. It depends on what we do whether liberal democracy has reached its end point. And we social scientists should provide accounts of this "doing." We need to bring agency back into our reflections on the long durée, as well as on the immediate future.

But as we bring agency back in, we should do so with care. Obviously, agency is constricted by circumstance, much of it inherited. Regularized patterns of social interaction, a.k.a. social structures and institutions, both facilitate and constrain our ability to act. The power of defining the situation is a key dimension of social life, but we enter situations that have been predefined. They point us in directions that are hard to turn or reverse, but they are nonetheless turned and reversed, intentionally and unintentionally. I think we must pay attention to how the turning and reversal happen.

This is the intellectual project of studying the social condition. The task of such inquiry is to illuminate the tensions in social life and the dilemmas they pose, life's questions, not to pretend that there are answers that lead to predetermined social structures and history. There is an understanding that how the dilemmas that are addressed, add up, with consequences that change the patterns of social interaction, i.e., structures and institutions.

As far as the adding up, I would point to the writings of Tarde as the thinker who thought of social persistence and social change in this fashion. As regards the tensions and dilemmas, the classical social theorist who explored this was Georg Simmel. Simmel understood that the metropolis, the modern city, is both a setting for loneliness and freedom, that money allows for individuation and domination, that social conflict both strengthens and weakens social order and change, presenting dilemmas, problems, and creative possibilities, beautifully rendered in his accounts of the conflicts and tragedies of modern culture.

More contemporary investigations get at this problem. In an unfortunately neglected volume, *Injustice*, Barrington Moore Jr., the author of the classic *Social Origins of Dictatorship and Democracy*, addresses the neglected problematic of when suffering and inequality come to be understood and acted upon as injustice, and the consequence for contemporary social arrangements and history. When do people accept and even justify their suffering, and when do they declare it to be unjust and act upon this declaration. Moore comes to my mind because these days I find myself focused on the problem of the difficult relationship between democracy and social justice.

But in fact, a great deal of normal social science inquiry proceeds with the social condition and uncertainty in mind. What I am proposing is a more explicit recognition of uncertainty, and a close examination of the way people deal with it.

Robin Wagner Pacifici's approach to "contingency in action" in *Theorizing the Stand Off*, is what I have in mind, as well as her earlier and later works. She has analyzed how participants in acute moments of conflict work through them with uncertain results and consequences: "events," concerning terrorism and the responses to it, surrender, radical urban politics, and much more. Less dramatic, but also pressing: Nina Eliasoph in examining "the politics of volunteering" shows how, built into the project of civil society activism, are numerous tensions between norms and ideals, and self-interests, and attempts to monitor the interaction between interests and ideals. Such tensions cannot be resolved, she suggests, but only worked through. And how they are worked is uncertain, but consequential. And Elżbieta Matynia in her study of performative democracy focuses on how people work to redefine the political situation and then puncture the apparent solidity of social structures and institutions through their dramaturgical performances. As they develop new scripts in their performances, the outcomes are unknown, but new possibilities are constituted.

I also would like to highlight that this perspective animates much of the research of many of my students, including, to name just a few: Nancy Hanrahan on music, Yifat Gutman on memory activism, Zachary Metz on "peace writ small" in areas of intractable conflict, Irit Dekel on mediation at the Holocaust Museum in Berlin, and Patrick Gilger on the public life in post-secular societies. I didn't realize it at the time I was directing their dissertations, but they all followed the project of illuminating the uncertainties of the social condition and accounting for how people deal with them. I was always careful to let students follow their own paths, but I think unintentionally I was fostering a group of young scholars with the common concern of exploring how people confront the uncertainties of social life.

And, indeed, almost all my study of culture and politics in Europe and the United States follows this logic as well. In fact, I admit, when I think of this general approach, I am reflecting on my work over the years, from Polish student theater to the project of *Reinventing Political Culture*. These studies are predicated on the ambiguities and ambivalences of modern social life. The *uncertainties* for better or worse. Donald Levine, my dissertation supervisor, and Robert Merton, as it happens the man who chaired my tenure review, opened the door for investigations along these lines. I think, bearing in mind our present circumstances, ambiguity and ambivalence should be investigated more fully. The acute nature of our present situation highlights the more general implication, both sociological and political.

Our present uncertainties are unsettling. Obviously, we can no longer count on the powers of science and medicine to save us when so many now are ignoring their genuine gifts. The pandemic continues to rage, and environmental disaster has become a normal aspect of daily life. But I do see a grounds for hope when thinking about democracy. Uncertainty challenges resignation. By embracing uncertainty, we are empowered to act, and we social scientists should illuminate this.

I am uncertain; therefore, I act, and appreciate others who act wisely.

3. Intellectuals in Dark Times: Reflections on Lived Experience

To act wisely, and to appreciate others who act wisely requires an understanding of our relationship with our compatriots. It requires an understanding of the role of intellectuals as we have facilitated different kinds of political movements and regimes. On April 11, 2023, I gave a talk at Indiana University on this topic. I did so by reflecting upon the way I have understood the democratic role of intellectuals at different times in my life. This chapter is adapted from the notes I prepared for that talk.

Over the past fifty years, I have wondered about the political roles of intellectuals in different political contexts. I've been thinking about this problem as a New Left radical, as an observer and analyst of the developing opposition to previously existing socialism around the Soviet bloc, with a focus on Poland, as a critic of "transitionology," the policy inquiry into the required steps to be taken in transitioning from dictatorship to democracy after the fall of Communism, and as a contributor to American public life. My life experiences have informed my intellectual journey and my scholarship, as these have informed my experiences.

I have come to two strong conclusions: intellectuals, people like you (dear reader) and me, can be especially dangerous, responsible for great suffering and devastation. But we also can play key roles in constituting and sustaining democratic life and achieving social justice.

Idealism, opportunism, fear, cowardice, and arrogance, built on a false sense of certainty, leads us to succumb to the tyranny of our own theories, to believe that we know better. And, based on what we think we know, we imagine a bright and beautiful future, imposing horrible conditions on the road to our imagined utopia. Czesław Miłosz's *Captive Mind* stands as a guide to the different ways this has come about.

I have also noted that the negative and positive roles of intellectuals are not a matter of good and bad intentions, of good and bad faith. To put it provocatively: some of my best friends and colleagues, often individually gentle and of good will, have had the potential to become monsters, and, in my judgment, it has been the case that American colleagues have avoided this fate only because of their marginality. I've known former Stalinists in Central Europe who, at the time of their enthusiasms, were not all that different from my American new left friends of the sixties and the true believers of recent years. Consider the biography of Zygmunt Bauman by Izabela Wagner to understand this.

I'm more specifically thinking of people who in this century have enthusiastically discovered the importance of democratic centralism, the discipline of the party, those who are enamored by their own theoretical imagination and enthusiastically denounce capitalism in ever more inventive new ways, Nancy Fraser's "cannibal capitalism" is the latest. I'm astonished how repeatedly it is asserted that all the problems of social and economic injustice, racism, sexism, and ecological disaster will be solved only if capitalism, (or is it neo-liberalism?) is abolished.

But my focus has not been on this dark side of intellectuals in politics, the way intellectuals have contributed to the darkness of our times. Rather, I have explored, and will explore with you, promise: the way intellectuals positively can enlighten and make contributions to the constitution of democracy.

I'll start with my reflections as an old new leftist, move on to my work in East Central Europe, and then onto my American publishing experiences, offering my reflections on my engagements in our public life.

But before I do, a few words on the key terms of this presentation: *intellectuals* and *dark times*.

Intellectuals: We share an implicit understanding of who we think of as intellectuals, I believe, revealed by key figures, Emile Zola on the unjust treatment of Dreyfus, Albert Camus and Jean Paul Sartre later in Paris, the New York intellectuals that Russell Jacoby saw passing, and the exiled intellectuals that Edward Said celebrates, as well as the dissidents around the old Soviet bloc, and in Russia, Cuba, Iran, and China today. Note: the role these people have played is not the same as that of scholar, academic, artist, scientist, policy analyst, or expert. Any one of these become an intellectual, we know intuitively, when they use their expertise, addressing the non-expert, a more general public, concerning pressing problems of the day.

On Dark Times: I am not just referring to bad times, but I turn to Hannah Arendt's conception—to times during which the problems and conditions of a political world are hidden, not visible, not capable of being politically examined, discussed, and addressed by a public, during which the public is diminished, times lacking illumination.

With this clarification in mind, I offer my thoughts on my experiences as a participant observer of such characters, intellectuals, in such times.

Reflections of an Old New Leftist

As a young man, I opposed the war in Vietnam before many of my friends and acquaintances. In high school in the mid-1960s, this led to some ostracism, but in college, my views became popular, I found myself in a Students for Democratic Society type group, ostentatiously named "The New Left Organizing Committee." We eventually led the 1970 protest against the American incursion into Cambodia and the protest against the killing of demonstrators at Kent State University in Ohio. We were really little more than a radical reading group, applying what we learned from our readings of Hegel, Marx, and Marcuse to what we saw as a profoundly unjust war, and racist society. The first class I ever taught at a university was in an alternative program we organized during a student strike at the State University of New York at Albany, my topic: Herbert Marcuse's "Critique of Repressive Tolerance."

Among my vivid memories during this time in my life are: that teaching experience, leading demonstrators in the thousands, shutting down the Federal building of New York state and stopping traffic on the New York State Thruway, protesting the war, and at a smaller demonstration, attempting to occupy the offices of the State Department of Corrections after the violent end of the revolt in Attica. And I remember being at a Free Bobby Seale rally in New Haven, facing the National Guard, overseen by hovering National Guard helicopters. Abbie Hoffman spoke, arguing for a thorough cleansing of American society, declaring "we all need a bath." My partner, Naomi Gruson, now my wife, used his declaration for a striking painting in her distinctive style. Jean Genet also gave a forceful speech.

His compatriot, Jean-Paul Sartre, was then my ideal intellectual. Armed with a superior understanding of history and the human condition, my comrades and I stood against oppression, fighting for justice. As is often said, "we spoke truth to power." Intellectuals, I understood then, use their critical knowledge to fight against the oppressive capitalist order, seeking to mobilize the masses, working for liberation. And intellectuals were not simply those with superior education and knowledge. They were those who used their knowledge to move the people, to change the world, to stop the oppressive powers of the state and of corporations. As Sartre dramatically put it: while Oppenheimer was not an intellectual when he developed the atom bomb, he was an intellectual when he fought against nuclear proliferation.

But even back then, I had some concerns.

I remember an incident during a strike at the university, following the American escalation of the Vietnam War with a systematic bombing campaign in Cambodia. We were marching around the campus at the State University of New York at Albany, "the quad," the sterile academic platform of neoclassical modernist buildings designed by Edward Durrell Stone. As I recall, it was the evening of May 4, 1970. Earlier that day, the Ohio National Guard shot and killed four Kent State students protesting the then recent escalation in the war. The demonstrators turned toward the university's library. I was shocked, perplexed, and became depressed. My fellow students trashed what I understood to be a sacred place. Shelved books were thrown to the ground. Enthusiastic shouts of mindless slogans echoed within the library's walls: "the people united will never be defeated," "oink-oink, bang-bang, ungawa people's power," "the revolution has come, time to pick up the gun, off the pigs!" and the like.

As the students entered the building, I observed an acquaintance swinging some sort of bat, kicking with her boots, breaking the glass panels of a door at the entrance to the building. I knew her to be more a hippie, a druggie, not a politico, not someone who thought much about the war in Vietnam and the struggles against injustice in the United States. "Politics weren't her thing." She "wasn't into politics." I knew her to have a difficult relationship with her parents. I knew her as a lovely, gentle, charming, but confused, young woman. I saw for the first time in my life in this acquaintance the manifestation of mob psychology, she a personification of the madness of the mob. She was one, publicly unknown, among many. Because I knew her, I was taken aback, am still taken aback.

This was at the beginning of the mass protests of the spring of 1970 in Albany, New York.

I noticed a pattern. The task for our group as the demonstrations escalated was to find meaningful targets of protest, but also to make sure that madness did not overwhelm and diminish the focus of the protests. We moved from small group of radical critics who came up with inventive ways to make our critical points, to a kind of police force, enforcing focus.

Three days before these events, at the New Haven rally, I was introduced to members of the Weather Underground. They were friends of the graduate student leaders of the New Left Organizing Committee. Years later, I realized that they may have been involved in the explosion steps away from the New School for Social Research, my academic home for over forty years, but back then I didn't have this more intimate tie.

I did have my doubts about them. The Weather Underground was using bombing to radicalize the American public, opposing the war in Vietnam abroad and social injustice at home, informed by a radical critique of American capitalism and neo-imperialism. They sought radical transformation, revolution. But I was perplexed about how this was supposed to unfold. When I participated in radical demonstrations, I was struck by the warm ties, the tight solidarity and enthusiasm among the activists, our expressive delight in our radical acts, but this strikingly contrasted with the antagonism of onlookers. This was notably different from my experience in broader demonstrations against the war, during which I sensed more support. The radical demonstrations made sense to us, but I was not sure whether they would accomplish anything other than alienate the broader public. And this was especially the case when it came to bombings and terrorist activities. I didn't know it then, but through my uncertainty, I was beginning to reconsider my understanding of the role of the intellectual, even the radical intellectual, in democratic society.

Reflections of an Expert of a System that No Longer Exists: Before the Fall

I started seeing things differently in the People's Republic of Poland. I went in 1973 believing that the socialism of my imagination had nothing to do with the so-called "socialism" of the Soviet Empire. I thought that it was a deformation of an ideal, looking for reasons why this was so: the emergence of a new class, the development of state capitalism, the backwardness of pre-Soviet Russia. But I came to realize that it wasn't so simple. That there was more of a connection than I had first wanted to believe. (I look back at my identity of those times as the period when I was a "wannabe Marxist.") But more importantly, for our purposes today, I started to pay close attention to the Central European intellectuals as dissidents to the official, prevailing, deeply flawed political regime.

The dissident intellectuals were not only against the powers that be, as my friends and I were in the United States. The way they opposed the powers was especially instructive, and in an important way an end in itself. Crucially important was their shift away from developing a singular alternative truth. They went beyond speaking truth to power. They held a diversity of opinions and judgments, had a variety of different primary concerns. Some were Marxist revisionist, others were anti-Communist, some were secular, others, Catholics. But their diverse commitments were not primary. Rather, they seemed to be dedicated above all else to constituting a democratic space for responding to the fundamental problems of the political order, in which people with different positions and sensibilities could meet, talk, and listen to each other, and develop a capacity to act together. Adam Michnik's book *Kościół, lewica, dialog* (The church, the left, dialogue) emphasized this commitment. To my disappointment the book was published in English as *The Church and the Left*. The key political commitment of the book was not in the title.

I saw this principle in practice first in alternative theaters, then in the democratic opposition, and then in *Solidarność*, the nationwide labor movement that became a broad social movement pitched against totalitarian rule in Poland.

Polish Student Theater: I went to Poland to do a comparative sociology of theater in New York City and in Warsaw. I was extending a preliminary study I conducted in New York City, working with my professor, Alicja Iwańska. In that study, I outlined the way that distance from the market mechanism of theater support in New York City opened up greater latitude for experimentation and political provocation, from Broadway to off-Broadway to off-off-Broadway. While the findings were not particularly surprising, my professors were impressed. And so were the judges of the International Research and Exchange Board, who decided to fund my proposal to extend my research to Warsaw, Poland.

Yet, once I was in Poland, I struggled for months to find meaningful comparisons. I tried but failed to design the study of theater in the city. Then, a professor of theater, Zbigniew Osiński, provided me with a lead. He informed me about an upcoming student theater festival in the city of Łódź. He thought these theaters might be what I was looking for, and he was right. When I attended, I did find confirmation of the pattern I outlined in New York. The theaters were far from the political center of Warsaw. They were not supported directly by the Party or the Ministry of Culture. The participants didn't depend on the political support of their artistic work to earn their keep. They were as distant from the primary steering mechanisms of the social and political order (the party state) as the off-off-Broadway theaters were from the logic of the market. But confirming the pattern was just the beginning.

Because the theaters I observed were so fascinating, I decided to focus on them and not the theater landscape in comparison with the American theater landscape. I decided to sociologically explain how it was that their artistic and political innovations and provocations were possible in a society directed and controlled by the Communist Party, to explore "art in repressive context," and to examine the sociological implications of this social fact and of their creative work. I embarked on a sociological study not only of theater, but also through theater, as I later explained in my job talk at the New School for Social Research. The works of the theaters themselves helped me hone my sociological and political approach. Dialogue, drama, paradox, and dilemma were key to the works of these theaters and key to my sociological approach to this day, informing my understanding of the role of intellectuals in dark times.

In retrospect, what I now take to be my central finding was one that I did not sufficiently analyze in my first publications, though it often came up in discussions I had about my work. I was observing the emergence and consequences of an alternative public life apart from the one that the party state was promoting and controlling, a public life that was constituted by young critical intellectuals, who suggested a different model for the role of the intellectual in a democratic movement or organization.

I remember vividly my encounters with Morris Janowitz, a member of my dissertation committee and a leading political and military sociologist, when I came back from my research and was starting to write my findings, and when I defended the work. Right away, he wanted to know whether the theaters I studied were for or against the regime. Were they Communist or anti-Communist? I tried to explain to him that there wasn't a simple answer to that question. Without clarity in answering this question, he didn't see their political significance. Later, at my dissertation defense, Janowitz forthrightly questioned my critique of the notion of a totalitarian society. He supported my work, but I couldn't convince him. I tried to explain that it wasn't the partisan position of the theaters that was most important, but the very fact that they existed despite official censorship, evading its controls. They created a free zone distinct from the public spaces more closely controlled by the regime, a space that included the work of neo-Marxists of sorts and of Catholics, and, to echo Adam Michnik's understanding of democracy, those who were just dedicated to "monkey business." Their existence belied the notion of a totalitarian society.

Others at the University of Chicago, my fellow PhD students particularly, were also puzzled by my study of these theaters. My topic seemed to be quite esoteric, even trivial, not a significant project for sociological investigation. Even the commencement speaker at my graduation ceremony highlighted the apparently esoteric aspect of my dissertation in her speech as indicative of the range of work done at the university. She quoted my title asking: what are "The Sociological Implications of Polish Student Theater"?—getting a good laugh.

This contrasted remarkably with the response I received from Poles and experts on Poland. They knew that there was something special about this theater, and they appreciated my analysis. These theaters were an archetypical example of independent public expression, indeed independent public life in a Communist society, as I put it in my one and only publication in the leading American sociology journal. The importance of this independence became clear in the years that followed my research for my dissertation, while I was defending it.

The Democratic Opposition and Solidarność: In the 1970s, Poland sunk into a deep economic crisis. In response, the Communist authorities sought an increase in the price of food and other necessities. Repeatedly, such a move led to labor unrest, in 1970, 1976, and 1980. As the decade opened there was a labor strike, sparked by the increase in the price of food, that was brutally repressed, but also led to a change in Party leadership and direction. Mid-decade, there was a protest among a group of prominent intellectuals concerning changes in the constitution that formalized the Communist Party's domination and subservience to the Soviet Union, followed by another workers' protest in response to the announcement of rising prices. Crucially, after these protests were repressed, a group of intellectuals made common cause with the workers, establishing the Committee to Defend Workers. As a result, the kind of embedded public life I observed in student theater effectively, though slowly, seceded from party-state direction and control.

An independent "Bulletin of Information" was published, with prominent intellectuals providing information on the workers who were being repressed, and creating a welfare fund for their defense and in support of their families. Other completely independent publications followed, the first, *Zapis*, a political-cultural publication of previously censored works, another *Robotnik*, a publication on workers' concerns, advocating independent workers' associations, and dozens of others, along with independent book publishing houses. All of this was not legal but persisted despite repression. Please note, the existence of a developed system of independent publishing was unprecedented in Communist-controlled societies. The creation of an oppositional public sphere was an extraordinary achievement, unimaginable before it happened.

The relationship between the intellectuals and the workers was strikingly different in this sphere than the one that conventionally was imagined by the Party vanguardist, along with other leftists. Intellectually derived theories of history, revolution, and transformation were not proposed. Rather, a mutually respectful dialogue developed. This laid the groundwork for the relationship between intellectuals and workers in the formation of *Solidarność*. The monologues of Sartre and the young radicals of the anti-war movement, such as my New Left Organizing Committee, were replaced by dialogues.

Intellectuals were brought in as advisors. Workers drew upon their experiences in the workplace—factory floors, shipyards, and steel mills. Intellectuals and workers shared their different experiences and insights, learning from each other and imagining a future together, and acting upon their learning and imaginations, and negotiating with the Communist authorities. A genuinely free public sphere emerged that radically changed the protests in the Gdansk region of 1980 into nationwide protests, leading to the first completely independent trade union in the Communist bloc. The workers revolted against the workers' state. Yet, the leader of the union, Lech Wałęsa, repeatedly asserted that the union was not politically challenging "the leading role of the Party." The union was creating independent public space for speech and action but was not directly competing with the regime for political domination.

My Summary Observations: In observing the creation of independent publics in the student theater, then the democratic opposition, and then *Solidarność*, I perceived the constitution of an independent public life in Polish society that became a force that ultimately contributed to the fall of the Soviet Empire. Such public formation was not the cause of the fall, to be sure. The inefficiencies of the Soviet-style socialist economy, the costs of the arms race, and the Soviet's Afghan misadventures, obviously all were factors. Nonetheless, the intellectuals' contribution to the constitution of a free and open public life was a factor, and crucially made it more likely that democracy had a chance after dictatorship and that the transformation would be achieved through peaceful means. The intellectuals' special democratic role was to foster the dialogue that made this possible. They crossed class lines. They bridged the divide between the secular left and a deeply religious general public. They were more interested in speaking and reforming each other, instead of speaking truth to power. It was an approach that Adam Michnik named "the new evolutionism" and Václav Havel coined as "living in truth."[10]

My Engagement: In the late 1970s and the 1980s I worked with such intellectuals, acting in this way. I even co-organized a semi-clandestine project in which this approach was enacted. In 1984, I traveled to Warsaw as part of a New School for Social Research delegation to present Michnik with an honorary degree for the work he had done in the democratic movement in Poland. We honored him for his work as an innovative democratic intellectual, for his bold intellectual insights, and for his brave political action. He was scheduled to receive his degree in New York as part of the ceremony commemorating the fiftieth anniversary of the establishment of the University in Exile at the New School, but was then imprisoned, for his underground Solidarity activities. Czesław Miłosz accepted the degree for Michnik in his absence.

Months later, he was released, and a small New School delegation hosted a ceremony for him in Warsaw in the spacious apartment of Edward Lipinski, the ninety-three-year-old socialist, turned Communist, turned patron of the democratic opposition. A who's who of the opposition was there, including most prominently Jacek Kuroń, in Michnik's mind his opposition teacher, who, after the fall of the Communist regime, became the Minister of Labor, and Bronisław Geremek, the most learned of the opposition intellectuals, a medieval historian of international renown, and after the fall, Poland's Minister of Foreign Affairs. After the ceremony, Michnik, Kuroń, Geremek, and I, joined Jonathan Fanton, the president of the New School, and Adrian DeWind, a member of our Board of Trustees and his wife, for a dinner in Warsaw's premier Hotel Victoria, stared at by the waiters and diners in the restaurant, no doubt along with a watchful secret police.

The week after the ceremony, as Michnik introduced me to many of his colleagues in the opposition, we had extended conversations. We talked about his support for Chilean copper miners, controversial in Poland because the miners were often Communist and the regime was steadfastly anti-Communist, about his appreciation of the Russian dissidents, about my opposition to Ronald Reagan, which amused him, and about books of mutual interest, especially the writings of Hannah Arendt, and specifically her *The Origins of Totalitarianism*.

On the last day of our week together, we visited Jan Józef Lipski, in a cardiac hospital in the far eastern edge of Warsaw. Because of his heart condition, Lipski couldn't go to Lipinski's for the award ceremony, so we went to this major historian of the left to celebrate. Walking from the hospital to the bus stop, Adam proposed to me, "now that we were New School for Social Research colleagues," a project of forming a seminar with our mutual friends in Czechoslovakia and Hungary, on the topic of democracy, starting with a discussion of Arendt's *Origins*. Our seminar functioned clandestinely until 1989 and then after extended all around the bloc, very much modeled after other independent public initiatives of the unofficial public sphere of those times. Thus, I not only had a front row seat to one of the major changes of the twentieth century, the collapse of the Soviet Empire and the project of creating a democratic aftermath to the fall, I had a bit part. I helped create a small independent international zone for critical reflection, which was dedicated to the key dialogic role of critical intellectuals. This smallness later became very instructive.

Reflections of an Expert of a System That No Longer Exists: After the Fall

We now know that the victory of the democratic opposition over Soviet Marxism and Communism did not signal a clear and decisive democratic happy ending, Hollywood style. Things didn't go all that well, and I must say that intellectuals were implicated. The problem, in my judgment, was epitomized by a famous book by a recent visitor to Bloomington, Francis Fukuyama's *The End of History*, but for me more personally it was revealed in my friendship and work with a distinguished Polish sociologist, Edmund Mokrzycki.

I met Edmund periodically in Poland in the 1980s, a respected professional who stayed clear of political engagement. We first met when I was working on my PhD and he was visiting the University of Chicago as a post doc in the early 1970s, the guest of the famous quantitative sociologist, James Coleman. Edmund's scholarship focused on the philosophical dimensions of social scientific methodology. He was a historian of sociological thought and an editor of the *Polish Sociological Bulletin*. He was a social scientist, not a politically engaged intellectual, during Communist times.

During those times, people such as Edmund played an important role. They kept the ideals of independent social scientific inquiry, apart from ideology, alive in Poland. He admired the engaged intellectuals in the opposition, but that was not his role as he understood it.

I admired him and vividly remember a dark, cold, cloudy day in November 1987 in a dark, underheated café in the Hotel Victoria, again along with Jonathan Fanton. There was a shortage of heating fuel and periodic electricity blackouts then. There was a stalemate between the repressive state and the opposition. Things were not working. Edmund then told me that he knew the present order of things could not last. This fundamentally apolitical man told me that perhaps he wouldn't see the collapse of Communism, but he was certain that his daughter, Olga, would. We saw this much sooner than he or anyone else expected.

With the collapse of Communism, Fukuyama was certain in his proposition that history had ended in the sense that liberal democracy and capitalism had triumphed ("they were the only game in town"). Following this logic, Edmund was of the mind that the times in Poland, and the other post-Communist nations, called for experts, such as himself, not intellectual critics. The course of these societies was set, in his judgment, informed by Fukuyama's sensibility if not his book. It was Edmund's sense that it was a time to work on the implementation of the set course. His time had come. Intellectuals such as Adam Michnik were no longer needed. His judgment reflected a general consensus, and it was this consensus, which also led to a literature on political, economic, and social transitions. I wrote my book *Civility and Subversion* in critical response. A recent book by András Bozóki[11] documents this turn of events.

I believe that this "end of history" consensus darkened the times. The notion of societal transition with a certain path from dictatorship to democracy seemed absurd to me. The need to critically examine the implemented transition policies, especially as they were having an impact upon, and were and were not understood by the general public, needed to be discussed.

It was and is my deep conviction that intellectuals still had and have important roles to play: to subvert dominant views that concealed the problems of the times, and to make it possible for those who oppose each other to talk to each other, i.e., the roles of civility and subversion (the title of my book on the role of the intellectual in democratic societies), provoking deliberation and common action to address the pressing issues of the times and enduring social problems. I used what I learned from Central European intellectuals to develop a criticism of developments on both sides of the old Iron Curtain. I came to this conclusion by reflecting on the actions of the oppositionists to the previously existing socialist order, but also by reflecting on the long history of intellectual practice, starting with reflections on the life and death of Socrates.

Intellectuals in the post-Communist period, both in the political West and East, needed to subvert what came to be known as the neo-liberal consensus. (I hate the term, but that's another story.) And they had to civilize discussion among political opponents, as "history" demonstrated that it had far from ended, particularly concerning such issues as the cultural, social, and political contradictions of capitalism, the enduring problems of racism, sexism, and the conflict among nations, the conflicts over the ecological crisis, and much else.

Around the former Soviet bloc, the well-educated young generally accepted the shock therapy prescribed by Western observers and consultants as the way to move from the highly inefficient and chaotic command economy of the previously socialist systems to a more rational one. For them, the idea of integration into Europe was highly attractive. Travel opportunities were greeted with glee, as their lives improved rapidly. But for less skilled, older people in the towns and in the countryside, the promise was great, but the improvements were minimal, at least initially. The technocratic response to the post-Communist changes did not speak for itself. There needed to be informed public discussion. Contrary to Edmund, I thought they were needed more than ever. Contrary to Fukuyama, it seemed to me that this was not the end but the beginning of history, in which citizens had a capacity to shape their future. Because public discussion was not as inclusive as it should have been, it has seemed to me, the public took a populist turn. Xenophobia and religious fundamentalism appealed, especially when linked to the condemnation of corruption and despair over growing inequalities. The need for informed dialogue and debate was greater than ever. I see echoes of this situation in the present crisis of liberal democracy, in the United States, Central Europe, and far beyond.[12]

And Then, as They Say, "9/11" Happened

Before September 11, 2001, the twentieth century seemed short, opening with the Bolshevik Revolution of 1917, closing with the fall of the Berlin Wall in 1989. After 9/11, the period between 1989 and 2001 appeared to be a twentieth-century postscript, with the same struggles and debates between the left and the right, capitalism and socialism, neo-colonialism and post-colonialism, democracy and dictatorship, and totalitarianism and open societies still ongoing, though some such as Mokrzycki and Fukuyama turned away from this. But after September 11, 2001, the dialogic terrain changed.

The attacks on the World Trade Center and the Pentagon appeared as the opening of the new century. Of course, the legacies of totalitarianism, colonialism, and the clear and present dangers of the dark sides of capitalism and socialism have been still with us, with a heightened understanding of the threats of environmental and nuclear catastrophes. But wise responses to all this is uncertain, for better (as was considered in the previous chapter) and for worse, and this has implications for the democratic vocation of intellectuals.

Grand gestures appeared hollow. Creative actions have illuminated hope.

After the attacks, I leaned on Arundhati Roy, the novelist, but not Arundhati Roy, the intellectual, the author of *The God of Small Things*, and not the public intellectual who grandly condemned the American response to the attacks on the Pentagon and the World Trade Center, where I lost one of my closest friends, Michael Asher.

On the big center stage, it hurt to think. I looked at alternative, more marginal, stages for hope. I reflected on my East Central European experience, at kitchen tables, alternative bookstores, and literary salons, and eventually the actions of *Solidarność* to understand the new stages appearing in the United States, meetup.com and moveon.org, especially as they linked with the presidential campaign of a doctor turned governor from the small state of Vermont, Howard Dean. Roy illuminated such a marginal stage in her account of the relationship between the hero of her novel, the untouchable "God of Small Things," and his upper-caste illicit lover. I go into this in detail in my books *The Politics of Small Things* and *Reinventing Political Culture*. But I want here to just emphasize the primary finding when it comes to the role of the intellectual in dark times.

Intellectuals can and do make a difference when they open up spaces, large and small, face to face, and digital, for the intelligent consideration of pressing problems of the day and also enduring problems of the human condition, when they constitute dialogue about less immediately apparent problems, and when they facilitate discussion among those who oppose each other who can't or won't engage each other. It seemed to me that the small became again especially significant, similar to the significance I found in Polish student theater behind the Iron Curtain decades before 9/11.

I couldn't support the attacks or accept those who saw some form of rough justice in them.[13] I also couldn't accept the Manichean declaration of a war on terrorism, nor those who focused on their opposition to the war on terrorism to the point that they ignored the abomination of the 9/11 attacks. But I saw in the making of the anti-war movement and its link to the campaign of Howard Dean, who claimed to represent the democratic wing of the Democratic Party, a hopeful alternative. I thought the primary significance of this campaign and its connection to the anti-war movement was the public space it opened for grounded, consequential discussion and concerted action that linked a social movement with an institutionalized political party.

This suggested to me a richer set of tasks for intellectuals in dark times, the way intellectuals can and do illuminate public life not only on the center stage but in various nooks and crannies, creatively using available media. They can make it possible for opponents to confront and talk to each other in a more informed and deliberate fashion, as they can work to subvert not only hegemonic common sense, that of so-called neo-liberalism, the war on terrorism, and the common sense defined by race, class, gender and sexual inequalities and injustices. But also, the more specific common sense of significant subcultures, as can be found in fragmented society. I have in mind here the problem of groupthink that can be found in universities and against universities in the battles most recently among the so-called woke, the anti-woke, and the anti-anti-woke, and in the pitched battles between those who identify as pro-Palestinian versus the pro-Israeli, those who are critical of the rising antisemitism on university campuses and those that use this antisemitism to attack institutions of learning in a new kind of McCarthyism, a new form of anti-intellectualism.[14]

Deliberately Considered, Public Seminar, and the Democracy Seminar

It was with such problems in mind that I started my experiments in online publishing, first with *Deliberately Considered*, and then in *Public Seminar* and *Democracy Seminar*. I tried to put into practice the findings of my years of research on intellectuals and the sociology of politics and culture, as these were informed by my public engagements.

Deliberately Considered started with a simple observation, then quite often ignored, that more and more political, cultural, and private life was developing online, and with a judgment:

that this presented both great opportunities and grave dangers. It opened public expression and discussion.[15] More people could express themselves and a broader range of perspectives could be expressed. Global conversations were becoming ever more possible, and it also became possible for "the politics of small things" to become large, very quickly, dramatically revealed in then new social movements of 2011—from the Arab Spring to Occupy Wall Street and much in between. In *Deliberately Considered*, we observed these developments for four years, as we tried to avoid some of the evident problems of the new media environment: a deluge of questionable information, the confusion of news with rumor, tendentious political argument that confuses rather than illuminates, intellectual gated communities rather than open intellectual exchange. The response of *Deliberately Considered* to all this is summarized by its name. We tried to slow things down a bit, adding serious thoughts about the events of the day, from a variety of different perspectives, theoretical positions, experiences, and places; from the left, right, and center; East, West, North, and South. Our final posts of the last week of its active publishing provides a clear overview of its project, which readers can find on the *Deliberately Considered* website.

In 2014, I suspended *Deliberately Considered* and formed *Public Seminar*, working with a group of New School colleagues. It was *Deliberately Considered* broadened to include colleagues across the university as contributors and editors, animated by the tradition of the founding of the New School in 1919 and the founding of the University in Exile in 1933, and informed by the work I, along with a group of colleagues, developed in the 1980s, supporting and learning from the circles of democratic intellectuals in East Central Europe, at first especially in Poland, Hungary, and Czechoslovakia. The online "seminar," in my understanding was an extension of a weekly seminar the German exiles conducted among themselves in the 1930s and continues in person to this day. Joining the seminar were not only my circles of friends and colleagues, but many others. At first, Public *Seminar* was a kind of small "mom and pop" operation, I was the editorial team; my wife, Naomi, published and distributed the work, very small indeed. Eventually many students and colleagues became actively involved, with Claire Potter and then Jim Miller joining me as executive editors, and to whom I later passed on the enterprise.

Also joining me was Indiana University's very own Jeffrey C. Isaac. With Claire Potter and Jeff, *Public Seminar* responded to the pressing problems of the day most beautifully with the publication of two books *#Charlottville* and *#Against Trump* (the latter a collection of Jeff's responses to the first year of Donald Trump's presidency).

We had an understanding of immense problems we were facing and the need for us to respond. We had no illusions that our modest publishing enterprise would change the world, but we did understand that if we could change a little corner of the world, it would be significant. This is the logic of my conception of the politics of small things. I drew upon that logic with Jeff and many others, including Adam Michnik, Elżbieta Matynia, and Shireen Hassim, and embarked on another online initiative: we relaunched *Democracy Seminar* in response to the ascendence of authoritarianism around the world at the party celebrating Jeff's book.

Democracy Seminar, Then and Now: When *Democracy Seminar* was established in the 1980s, the collaboration between the political East and the political West was asymmetrical. Our colleagues in East Central Europe faced systematic repression, while those of us in the United States and the political

West did not, even though we were critical of the limitations of liberal democracy as it existed. Such an asymmetry no longer exists. The threat of various forms of authoritarianism is global. We know that in some sense we are all in the same boat. The revived *Democracy Seminar* was dedicated to understanding the threat and considering ways of addressing it. We were committed to developing critical, on the ground, analyses and reports on the nature of and responses to the crises in democracy in the United States, East and Central Europe, and Latin America, concerning such issues as the problems of racism, gender and sexual inequality, the problems of populism, and much more. I am especially proud of our ongoing posts on the war on Ukraine and a symposium we published on illiberal democracy. We conducted webinars on such topics as media and democracy in Africa, populism, the 2020 election in the United States, and crucially for me two webinars with colleagues at the American University of Afghanistan (AUAF) just before the victory of the Taliban, and just after. This eventually led me to take a position at AUAF, where I have taught courses on civic engagement, democracy, and the politics of small things.[16]

Conclusion

I have developed my understanding of the democratic role of intellectuals both as a participant in and analyst of public life from Albany to Afghanistan. My experiences in East Central Europe were particularly important in coming to my understanding of the proper roles for intellectuals. I started as a radical leftist, and I became a radical centrist. I thought the responsibility of the intellectual was to speak truth to power, armed with a correct understanding of history, drawn from a careful understanding of powerful social theories. The task was to lead the masses, to create a popular movement against the forces of injustice. I learned the dangers of this position, understanding that while it sometimes is imperative, it often made matters worse. I saw signs of this even during my student radical days, but it became most apparent when I went to Europe. I learned the primary importance of a free and open public life, how it could be a powerful means to an end, and how it fostered a just end. I came to my position through my political experiences and also through reading. Hannah Arendt became my primary guide, to whom I now turn.

4. Hannah Arendt and the Radical Center

Of all my readings, Hannah Arendt's work has been my primary guide in understanding the theoretical underpinnings of my commitment to the radical center. In this chapter, I explain how I have come to learn from her. The chapter is based on a talk I gave in Brasilia in 2006 at a conference on Arendt's philosophy. My talk entitled "Hannah and Me" told the story of my relationship with her as a teacher, how reading her work provided the key to my understanding of the significance of the democratic opposition to Communism in East Central Europe, and of my understanding of politics more generally. I reached a set of conclusions that I believe cogently applied to the moment and underscored the political significance of a gray is beautiful sensibility and of the radical center. Here in a postscript to the lecture, I present an update applied to the challenges of our present circumstance.

Contrary to the suggestion of my original, rather informal, title, I did not study with Hannah Arendt, nor were we ever colleagues, although I missed both experiences only by a bit. I was a graduate student in the early 1970s in one of the universities where she last taught, the University of Chicago, and my first and only long-term position, at the New School for Social Research, was her primary American academic home. But when I was a PhD candidate, she was feuding with her department chair in the Committee on Social Thought, Saul Bellow, (or at least so it was said through the student grapevine), and she was, thus, not around. And I arrived at the New School one year after she died. Nonetheless, she was with me as an acquaintance at the University of Chicago, and soon after I arrived at the New School, we in a sense became intimates.

A Personal Story

At the University of Chicago, my dissertation included a critique of the notion of totalitarian society. Thus, I read both *On Revolution* and *The Origins of Totalitarianism*. From the point of view of Arendt scholarship, the effects of these readings were minimal. From *On Revolution*, I came to understand her point about the difference between the French and the American revolutionary traditions, giving me insights into the Soviet tradition, but this barely affected my thinking. From *The Origins*, along with other works, I came to an understanding of the totalitarian model of Soviet society, a model that I rejected.

But then I went to the New School, and in the spring of 1980, I came to appreciate Arendt in a much more serious way. A student kept on asking odd questions in my course on political sociology. I would use key concepts, and he repeatedly challenged my usage. "Society," "ideology," "power," "politics," "authority," "freedom"—I would use the terms in conventional social-scientific ways, and he would question me as an Arendt student, from me: society as a unit of human association; for him: society as the confusion of the public and the private. I understood ideology as a distinctive metaphoric system that makes an autonomous politics possible (Geertz student that I was). He saw ideology as a specific historical development, a special type of modern thinking and of doing politics that connected past, present, and future, and when linked with terror, *the* cultural component of totalitarianism. I understood power, politics, and authority, as all involving the interplay between culture and coercion, based in the latter; for him, careful distinctions should be made, showing that political power, based in freedom, is the opposite of coercion. I soon realized what was going on, and although he very much challenged my authority as a young assistant professor (thirty-one at the time), teaching in a graduate course in which many of the students were both older than me and quite sophisticated, I was intrigued. What he was talking about suggested a way to understand something I was observing that I knew wasn't properly appreciated.

The following summer, I read just about all of Arendt's published works. I was especially moved by her approach to the problems of the public and her conceptualization of politics as the capacity for people to act in concert. This was an unusual time in my life, an unusual time in contemporary politics. The darkness of the twentieth century was being lightened from the margins, and only a few were able to see it.

I was then observing the beginnings of major transformations in the political landscape that were developing in Poland, but not yet broadly recognized. From this century, I can say now that I was observing the forces that ultimately led to the peaceful collapse of the Soviet Empire. When Arendt wrote about dark times, she referred to the era of modern tyranny, of the totalitarianism of the Nazi and Stalinist regimes. This was a time when the illumination of public acts was dimmed. She observed that:

> It is the function of the public realm to throw light on the affairs of men by providing a space of appearances in which they can show in deed and word, for better and worse, who they are and what they can do, then darkness has come when this light is extinguished ...[17]

But, she also noted that:

> even in the darkest of times we have the right to expect some illumination, that such illumination may well come less from theories and concepts than from uncertain, flickering, and often weak light that some men and women, in their lives and their works, will kindle under almost all circumstances and shed over the time span that was given them on earth ....[18]

She celebrated the acts of great individuals who shed such light in her book *Men in Dark Times*. In everyday actions (as I demonstrated in the previous chapter), I saw in Poland the constitution of an alternative public space for such appearance in an emerging opposition movement that was then rapidly developing, leading a few months later to the establishment of *Solidarność*, the first independent union, the broad societal movement, constituting a free and open public space in a totalitarian order.

Yes, after my summer reading, I gave up on my critique of the totalitarian model, or more precisely, I refined it. I came to understand that although there can be no totalitarian society, that there were totalitarian movements and regimes, and their oppositions, and that sometimes the oppositions come in the form of heroic individuals, what Arendt wrote about, but at other times they took on broader public form. Her postscript to *The Origins* on the Hungary of 1956 was my guide. Hannah and I, then, became very close.

Arendt was with me as I went off to understand what was happening in "the other Europe," as Philip Roth would name it. In that Europe, in small interactions, big things were happening. People met each other and formed spaces of appearance apart from party-state definition. They spoke and acted freely in each other's presence, revealing themselves and constituting alternative public spaces. They did so in theaters, in underground publications, in independent unions (first very small, after 1980, nationwide), in unofficial literary salons, bookstores, and clubs. As I observed these developments, Arendt was my guide. With her guidance, I understood that the end of the activities of the opposition was to create a public space. That the question of whether the activities would lead to reform of the system (no one imagined its collapse) was really secondary. The constitution of a free public space was primary. That was the major transformation itself. It made it possible for people to be free. It provided dignity. And it created power that clearly would be consequential, although the exact consequences were unknown.

And as I have already explained, when Adam Michnik and I agreed to create a semi-clandestine *Democracy Seminar* based at the New School in New York with branches in Warsaw and Budapest, our first reading was *The Origins*. The three groups each read the book and discussed it. The discussions were recorded, and the proceedings exchanged.

At the time, there was an everyday mundane feeling about these activities. But after the fact, it is clear to me that they were truly revolutionary. They were little gems of the lost revolutionary tradition that Arendt wrote about, and they speak to our present circumstances. This is what I have been working on for decades now. Arendt's guidance endures.

So let's fast forward for a moment, to the newer configuration of dark times,[19] remembering Arendt's counsel, "Dark times ... are not only not new, they are not a rarity in history, although they were perhaps unknown in American history ...." From the point of view of New York, the United States is an exception no longer. "Darkness has come when this light [of the public] is extinguished by 'credibility gaps' and 'invisible government,' by speech that does not disclose what is, but sweeps it under the carpet, by exhortations, moral and otherwise, that, under the pretext of upholding old truths, degrade all truth to meaningless triviality."[20]

I have been thinking about this since the days immediately following the attacks of 9/11, thinking that led to the publication of *The Politics of Small Things: The Power of the Powerless in Dark Times*. I try to accomplish a number of different goals in my small book, which I attempted to very compactly express in its title. I have already explained quite a bit in this presentation.

I have a feeling that, in Arendt's sense, we do again live in dark times, but that they are different from the ones she knew. There are again struggles between gigantic forces of good and evil, in which both sides, moving both between East and West (think the war on terrorism), or North and South (think Chavez and Bush), darken the spaces of appearance. But I also think that to appear, speak to each other, develop a capacity to act together, as theorized by Arendt, but also as described by Václav Havel, the former Czech dissident and president, in his greatest work *The Power of the Powerless*, presents an alternative, a still significant "politics of small things." And that its power can be formed in everyday interactions, both face to face interactions and virtual ones using the new media.[21]

Mine is an attempt to find the men and women in dark times who present alternatives. I do this by using the work of Arendt and Erving Goffman to explain how the grand narratives of terror and anti-terror are not the only or even the most effective ways to address the pressing problems of our times. Terrorism is not the only weapon available to the oppressed, and militarized anti-terrorism is not the only or even the most rational way to fight the very real dangers of terrorism. I can obviously not make the case here. What I would like to do is to look at some details of the argument, as Hannah is with me. In that I am looking at micro interactions as the location for alternatives to the oppressions of the new grand narratives, the key theoretical issue is how can we tell when micropolitics is really an alternative, and when it is a sort of enactment of disciplinary powers of one larger regime or another. In my book, this problem presented itself as I attempted to show that the micropolitics of the Christian right and the anti-war left and the Dean campaign in the United States were not just presenting competing partisan positions in 2004 during the presidential elections. The alternative was between a new and efficient authoritarian unfreedom and a new and promising free democratic politics. To get at the issue and to the theoretical center of my presentation today, I propose we look at the way Arendt explains the relation between truth and politics, and the way Michel Foucault postulates the relationship between truth and power. Let me be forthcoming, I do not think that they present competing positions accounting for the same thing, but complementary accounts of two very different, even opposite phenomena.

Alternative Frameworks: Michel Foucault and Hannah Arendt

Foucault analyzes the problem of knowledge and power as the problem of the truth regime. Truth is a production of social practices and their discourses. It produces power and is controlled by it. There is no distance between truth and the powers. There are alternative powers with alternative truths. Foucault explains: "It is not a matter of emancipating truth from every system of power (which would be a chimera, for *truth is already power*) but of detaching truth from the forms of hegemony, social, economic, and cultural, within which it operates at the present time." The analytic task is to explore truth regimes. The critical task is to do the "detaching." The people developing the alternative publics around the old Soviet bloc, thus, can be understood as engaging in this sort of bodily detachment. But what is the value of it? Why choose one truth regime over another? Foucault does not explain. Arendt is critically suggestive in answering just these questions, as was my experience in the 80s. Now I will try to explain the crucial reason why she was such a help back then and how she provides a guide now.

Arendt maintains that there are two fundamentally different types of truth, factual versus philosophical truth, which have two very different relationships to political power. Factual truth (which is not part of Foucault's scheme) must be the grounds upon which a free politics (which is also not part of Foucault's scheme) is based. Philosophical truth must be radically separated from politics, the possibility of which Foucault denies. Her distinctions are made to facilitate an understanding of the nature of totalitarianism and its alternatives. This is crucial for the present inquiry, both for scholarly and for normative reasons. It centers on the constitution of public freedom and the possibilities of a democratic culture. Such constitution and possibility exist in and through the domain of a free public. While Foucault cannot distinguish between totalitarianism and liberalism, Arendt reveals how in the relationship between truth and power this crucial distinction is made. And we can thus recognize dark times and places, and also recognize the sources of light as alternatives.

In order to make the contrast between the two different types of truth clear, Arendt reflects upon the beginning of World War I. The causes of the war are open to interpretation. The aggressive intentions of Axis or the Allies can be emphasized, as can the intentional or the unanticipated consequences of political alliances. The state of capitalism and imperialism in crisis may be understood as being central. Yet, when it comes to the border of Belgium, it is factually the case that Germany invaded Belgium and not the other way around. A free politics cannot be based on an imposed interpretation. There must be an openness to opposing views. But a free politics also cannot be based on a factual lie, such as the proposition that Belgium's invasion of Germany opened World War I. Modern liberal democracy requires a separation of politics from philosophical truth, but it must be based upon factual truths, in order for those who meet in public to share a common world in which they can interact politically. In modern tyranny, factual truth is expendable as a matter of principle, while the tyranny is based on a kind of philosophical truth, an ideology, an official interpretation of the facts. When Arendt highlights Trotsky as a kind of totalitarian everyman in *The Origins*, she observes that he expresses his fealty to the truth of the Communist Party. But that he could be airbrushed out of the history of the Bolshevik Revolution, contrary to the factual truth that he was a key figure, commander of the Red Army, second only to Lenin, also is definitive of totalitarianism. This is the real cultural ground of political correctness, of official truth. The purported scientific understanding of the history of the Party substitutes for the political confrontation, debate, and deliberation. It is enforced by terror. As Hannah and I traveled around the old bloc and as we spoke and acted with our opposition colleagues, we were involved in attempts by social actors to free themselves of the official truth and to ground themselves in the factual truth.

From the point of view of Foucault, or, for that matter, from the point of view of the sociology of knowledge and culture, there is much that is unsatisfying about Arendt's position. The distinction between fact and interpretation, which she insists upon, is in practice hard to maintain, and empirically it is hard to discern. But this is not the telling point from Arendt's point of view. Rather, it is that the distinction needs to be *pursued*, so that a free public life can be *constituted*. A democratic public cannot be constituted if political questions are answered philosophically, nor can its citizens interact freely, speak and act in the presence of each other, if the grounds of their interactions are based upon state-imposed lies.

The politics of race in America cannot proceed democratically if a politically correct standard of racial interaction were actually imposed. (This is, of course, far from the case, given the popularity of critics of political correctness.) But, just as well, a democratic confrontation of the legacies of racial injustice in the United States could not proceed if the school texts instructed the young that Blacks owned whites, rather than the other way around. For a free public life to exist, there needs to be space for speech and actions based upon different opinions, then the people, and not the theorists, philosophers, historians, or scientists, can rule. And their rule can proceed on solid grounds if they share a political world together, which has some factual solidity.

The politics of truth is in the interaction. Factual truth is the bedrock of a free politics. Difference of interpretation and opinion is its process. That the factual sometimes fades into the interpretive does not mitigate against the requirement that an interpretive scheme or doctrine cannot substitute for politics. That the interpretive sometimes seems to the convinced to be the factual does not mitigate against the requirement that for people to meet and interact in a free public, they must share a sense of a factual world. That fact and interpretation get mixed up is very much a part of the messiness of politics, a messiness, which is confronted in concrete interactive situations. This points us in Goffman's direction, a direction I can't go into here. For now, we need to consider a bit more closely Arendt's position so that the historical context of our inquiry can be understood.

When Arendt first presented her diagnosis, the central critical thrust of her work involved her identification of the National Socialism of Germany with Soviet Communism. Although using traditional political categories, these regimes appeared to be opposites, one of the right and the other of the left, she underscored that in their use of ideology and terror, in their mode of governance, in their projects of total control, their similarities were much more important than their differences. They were regimes systematically organized to eliminate a free public life (her and my central normative concern, i.e., what I am naming here the radical centrist position). While the *Origins* can be read as a "dialectic of the enlightenment" with the teleology taken out, it is also an account of the destruction of free public space in political life. Arendt presents a sort of decline and fall of public life or as Richard Sennett has put it, a story of "the fall of public man." Her story of decline and fall takes the reader from the heights of antiquity to the depths of totalitarianism.[22]

She starts with her classical ideal. Pre-Socratic Greece represents for her the time when freedom beyond necessity flourished in the polis:

> The Greek polis once was precisely that "form of government" which provided men with a space of appearances where they could act, with a kind of theater where freedom could appear .... If, then, we understand the political in the sense of the polis, its end or *raison d'etre* would be to establish and keep in existence a space where freedom as virtuosity can appear. This is the realm where freedom is a worldly reality, tangible in words which can be heard, in deeds which can be seen, and in events which can be talked about, remembered, and turned into stories before they are finally incorporated into the great storybook of human history.[23]

The history of Western thought, for Arendt, is the history of the decline of the appreciation of this ideal situation, with catastrophic consequences in modernity. The Greek turn to political philosophy meant that the philosopher, the intellectual in contemporary language, sought to substitute the truth for political governance. The Christian identification of freedom with free will turned freedom into a private and not a public matter. This confusion of public and private, from Arendt's point of view, explains the identification of freedom with sovereignty as articulated by such thinkers as Hobbes and Rousseau, the argument in her essay "What is Freedom?". Structurally, this is manifest with the rise of society, as the place where she sees the public and the private confused as a matter of principle, a central theme of her *The Human Condition*. Modernity intensified this loss of a distinctively political capacity; even as independent democratic and republican political forms were invented. Arendt notes, with approval, the Anglo-American conception of political party, especially as defended by Edmund Burke. Competing parties presented alternative notions of the common good. Continental parties serving the interests of particular classes, she understands as movements that confuse the particular interests with the public good, the interests of property, real and capital, and the interests of labor, rural and urban, with the interests of the public. *Anti-Semitism, Imperialism* and *Totalitarianism*, the three parts of the *Origins*, each involve developments that destroy political capacity, as they are central to the history of European civilization. Totalitarian movements and regimes are the culmination of this story of radical depoliticization.

Arendt argues that what is distinctive about totalitarianism is its unique conflation of culture and coercion, ideology and terror.[24] The problem with her position is that it requires what appear to be utopian beliefs about the relationship between truth and politics: that interpretive truth and politics can be radically separated and that the factual truth can be the basis of politics. While her critique of the substitution of philosophy for politics may be cogent, and while it may be crucial for intellectuals and artists not to confuse their insights and imaginations for democratic deliberation and decision, her ideas about the separation of politics from truth may still seem unrealistic. Every political movement after all has its ideology, it can be observed.[25] Further, it is quite unclear how to maintain this separation while maintaining a commitment to factual truth. In these postmodern times, we are very much aware that one person's interpretation is another's factual truth. Indeed, the sociology of knowledge, at least since Mannheim, points in the same direction. It would seem that Foucault with his ideas about truth regimes is on the empirical mark. Yet, as I have already tried to demonstrate, there is a normative problem with Foucault's position. He cannot distinguish between Trotsky and Wilson, between a totalitarian and a liberal. Further, there are also empirical grounds for rejecting the completeness of the Foucaultian position.

This is where small things matter. It is a question of appearances, working to sustain realities. Truth and politics, knowledge and power, do not have a general relationship in modernity, as Foucault maintains. Rather, as we have already noted, social agents constitute the relationship in concrete interactive situations. The authorities of the old bloc tried to maintain an ideological definition of the situation. They did conflate knowledge and power. They presented an official truth and demanded that people appeared to follow its edicts. But in the alternative publics in the Soviet order, the imposed relationship was questioned. In official space people pretended to believe the official ideology, but they found places where it could be questioned.

Around the kitchen table among people, something I explore closely in *The Politics of Small Things*, in small gatherings of close friends and relatives, the pretense was dropped. People presented themselves to each other in a different guise. They constituted a clandestine public space where they could speak and act together, free of the demands of officialdom. A real escalation of the struggle against the official order was evident when this hidden space of free interaction came out into the open. Foucault would explain this development in a sort of value-neutral way. One truth regime, that of dissidents, was emerging from another. Perhaps, we would even want to go so far as saying that the regime of the new hegemonic order of globalization could be observed in the detaching of embodied practices from the truths, that is the ideology, of the old regimes. Note how much more we observe using Arendt as our guide.

In the positions of Foucault and Arendt, we observe two distinct understandings of political culture, two different ways of understanding the relationships between power and knowledge, truth and politics. While both get us beyond the lazy use of stereotype, for example, all Russians seek a strong central authority, Americans are flexible, the British are more formal, the French more rational, (Brazilians are not quite modern?), etc., they do so with very different formulations. Where Foucault sees an identity, Arendt sees a variable relationship. For Foucault, political culture is about truth regimes, about the particular way that power and knowledge are united. For Arendt, political culture is about how and how far power and culture are distinguished and related. I think both analytic approaches provide insights into important aspects of political experience.

In fact, I am not sure that we could decide which one is more accurate. Foucault reveals an important part of the story, generally not sufficiently appreciated. The powers are revealed and operating in the activities of daily life and there is a form of knowledge that both accounts for this and makes it difficult to inspect critically. Knowledge and truth discipline. But there are different kinds of truth, and they have different relationships with power and politics, Arendt forcefully maintains. This is a critique of Foucault's position, but more significantly, it highlights a domain that Foucault ignores. The political implication of this is great. It means that there is a domain for freedom which Foucault does not recognize. This provides the grounds for normative judgment, making it possible to contrast tyranny with freedom. It makes it possible to discern real alternatives in dark times. It illuminates the position of the radical center.

Seeking Light in Dark Times: Then and Now

In 2006, I concluded my talk with the following summary of what I had learned in my political travels with Hannah Arendt, pointing to some implications as they had shaped my research:

- After being confronted by my student, I learned to think about politics differently and appreciate the significance of the democratic opposition in East Central Europe as it was developing. It then became possible to understand that a major political power was emerging in opposition to totalitarianism, that this power was based on simple interactions of people set apart from the official order. A small example is the *Democracy Seminar* I took part in. The large and historically significant example was *Solidarność*. There was back then the confrontation between the totalitarian and the free world, between socialist and progressive forces and the forces of capitalism, between the geopolitical forces of good and the Evil Empire, but the political transformation from within the old order came from a political force not recognized in the grand clash, however it was depicted. It was a political force in Arendt's sense.

- This suggests a different way to think about our present darkness, about the world of the war on terrorism and the world of globalization. It suggests that we need to look at what I call a politics of small things as it presents alternatives to terrorism and anti-terrorism, to globalization and anti-globalization. Terrorism is not the only way for the weak to resist. And militarized anti-terrorism is not the way to meet the threat of the terrors of fundamentalism (of all sorts). Politics, in Arendt's sense, stands as an alternative.

- This led me to analyze how the internet, as a domain for politics, has been used by opposition forces to the war on terror in American politics. I analyze this in *The Politics of Small Things* through an ethnography of the virtual politics of the Dean campaign and the anti-war movement.

- And it has led me to continue my journeys in darkness with Hannah. I am spending time, with colleagues in the Middle East, trying to identify alternative political forces, in the Palestinian territories and Israel, in special places where Palestinians and Israelis meet as equals, speak and act in the presence of each other, revealing themselves, and creating the capacity to act together, doing politics in dark times, in the heart of darkness.

Now: The last point highlights a road that I regret was not taken, a result of lack of capacity, not of will. Around the same time that I gave the lecture in Brazil upon which this chapter is based, I was trying to form a collaborative research project on the politics of small things in Israel-Palestine, working with colleagues in Israel and in the occupied Palestinian territories, as well as with scholars from the region working in New York. We took preliminary steps, agreeing to explore and help cultivate zones of the politics of small things beyond the intractable century long conflict among Israelis and Palestinians.

Reading the relevant literature and observing daily life, I saw how people in the region struggled to work with each other in their daily lives, maintaining their dignity and principles, among taxi drivers at Israeli checkpoints, in dissident activities among hardened Palestinian and Israeli combat veterans, and among families who have lost loved ones to the wars, acting in concert to find ways to resolve their differences peacefully for their mutual security and in pursuit of justice. But putting together a group of scholars on both sides to study such activities proved to be beyond my abilities. It required working with Palestinian and Israeli academics, when there was reluctance among Palestinians to collaborate, given their commitment to boycott official Israeli institutions. A group of colleagues in Ramallah hesitantly considered ways to get around these difficulties. I think it would have been possible if I had had the necessary mastery of the culture and language. But I didn't. What I was equipped to do in East Central Europe, I couldn't do in the Middle East. Given what has happened since then, I profoundly regret I couldn't pull this off.

Yet, aided by Arendt, I continue to think about this project that failed. Her reflections on the promise and perils of Zionism have been particularly illuminating, writings that predate her major works, written in the 1940s.[26] I find her writings informative, not because she had the answers, but because she made acute observations and asked salient questions. She faced the tensions built into the project of creating a space for Jewish security and dignity in the immediate aftermath of the Holocaust, reflecting upon the past and the future of Zionism, as well as the past and future of Palestinian Arabs, which inspires me to do the same in the 2020s. Reading these texts is disorienting. Their saliency is striking. She was not clairvoyant, but simply described striking problems of those times that most ignored, very much like what is happening now.

In implicit debates between Bernard Lazarre and Theodor Herzl at the turn of the nineteenth to the twentieth century, she saw the tension between a politics based on the ideals of universal justice, with a politics based upon self-defense, with assertions about the universality of antisemitism. Reading this, I recognize the criticisms and the justifications for the Israeli response to the Hamas attacks of October 7, 2023.

Observing the Zionist meetings and resolutions of the time, she noted how the aspirations for a Jewish homeland became the political and military project of constituting a sovereign Jewish nation-state, and cogently spells out the likely dark consequences. Her concerns have been tragically confirmed over time, leading step by step to the war crimes in Gaza and brutalities in today's West Bank.

Arendt recognized that geopolitical resolutions of the conflict developed by what she called "the great powers" are likely to fail if the parties of the conflict don't recognize and seek to understand each other. And she cogently understands that the problem of antisemitism would not be solved with the establishment of Israel as a Jewish state, fearing that it may in fact intensify, both for those in Israel and in the diaspora. This insight has been darkly demonstrated in recent months.

I originally read these essays years ago. I don't remember exactly when; likely it was as I was imagining the project of the politics of small things in Israel-Palestine. As I am crafting this manuscript, I see them in a new light. Not only do they support the form of the politics of small things in seeking a way out of the tragedy. She recognized the kibbutzim and Hebrew University as possible bases of an alternative to the politics of sovereignty of the nation-state. She also illuminates the beauty of the gray and the importance of a radical center when confronting the social condition of the people who live side by side, even if not together, in Israel-Palestine, "from the river to the sea."

Arendt knew what too many of my myopic pro-Palestinian and pro-Israeli colleagues, friends, neighbors, and family, the radical Zionist and anti-Zionist coalitions, ignore. In Arendt's words: "The idea of Arab-Jewish cooperation, though never realized on any scale and today seemingly farther off than ever, is not an idealistic day dream but a sober statement of fact ...." She saw such cooperation as a key to the survival of a Jewish homeland for the survivors of the Shoah, a pressing necessity at that time, and she further thought that it had powerful potential in a postcolonial world order. "Indeed, the working out of such *modus vivendi* might in the end serve as a model of how to counteract the dangerous tendencies of formerly oppressed peoples to shut themselves off from the rest of the world and develop nationalist superiority complexes of their own."[27]

Then, as now, Zionists have sought a sovereign Jewish nation-state, differing among themselves only on the question of its borders, and the anti-Zionists absolutely opposed such a state. Both sides have had good reasons for holding their positions. Given the Jewish experience in Europe over centuries, culminating in the Holocaust, and given increasingly anti-Jewish sentiment and actions in the Arab world, and later in the Soviet Union, a safe space of refuge for world Jewry has been understood as imperative, including by Arendt. But on the other hand, Palestine should be the land for its long-term inhabitants, and their expulsion has been an abomination, a fundamental injustice. Palestinian Arabs should not have to pay for European sins. In this conflict, Arendt recognized the beauty of the gray, its radical potential and the fundamental importance of a public space to explore the gray possibilities, the fundamental importance of the radical center.[28]

5. Art After Auschwitz

*The conflict in the Middle East, then and now, is a matter of grays, not black and white. Arendt understood this as a political actor and thinker, as a Jewish refugee from Nazi Europe, living in the United States, looking at the contested land in the Middle East. More than is generally recognized, her reflections on her identity shaped her later work. In our terms, Arendt's recognition of the need to address the just claims of Palestinian Jews and Arabs in the 1940s required an appreciation of the beauty of the gray and her commitment to the politics of the radical center. In this chapter, based on a lecture I gave at the University of Virginia on February 28, 2017, entitled, "To Write Poetry after Auschwitz is (**NOT**!) Barbaric," I show how art works to support this, opening possibilities for dialogue, confronting the challenges of our dark times, long after the horrors of the twentieth century. I consider the consequences of this support first before and then after the ascendence of Trump and the challenges of twenty-first-century authoritarianism. Please note, the argument here is not that all art is politically gray, far from it, but that art, because it is not reducible to politics, opens possibilities for confronting the un- or under-examined, beyond clichés, often using a provocatively stark black and white palate, and even more often using vivid colors. Art is radically centrist.*

I am very pleased to join you today and share my reflections on the importance of art, not only poetry, as it helps us confront the social condition of collective memory in dark times. I am especially grateful for Irit Dekel's invitation to give this presentation. First, as my former student and now as a respected colleague and dear friend, she has taught me a great deal about the dilemmas of remembering after barbarism, my topic today.

I open by disagreeing with Theodor Adorno's proposition about art and the Holocaust: "To write poetry after Auschwitz is barbaric." (I am not sure that this is actually a disagreement with Adorno as a thinker, just with his startling provocation.) I judge that, contrary to Adorno's infamous declaration, art after modern barbarism is imperative, though as Irit has demonstrated in her work, this is a messy, complicated business, complications that my friend and colleague, Jeff Olick, also here, has contributed a great deal in illuminating. What I most like about Jeff and Irit's work is that they both confront the social condition, as it applies to memory.

I will support my judgment here about art after Auschwitz, by exploring how specific works of art have made it possible to confront difficult pasts, helping their creators and their publics to confront the problem of memory and forgetting. Indeed, I will show that it is exactly in significant works of art that difficult pasts are addressed with nuance and creativity, moving their audience beyond clichéd reflection, enriching public memory, and opening more promising relationships between the past and the future.

Since this is not a soap opera, with a melodramatic ending, allow me to summarize the argument you are about to hear. Reflecting on three major works of art, I show that art informs memory beyond clichés. It illuminates the social condition of memory, the inevitable dilemmas of remembering some things, while forgetting others. Art does not provide easy lessons, but questions and presents alternative understandings and commitments. Enriching collective memory, Toni Morrison's *Beloved*, Pawel Pawlikowski's *Ida*, and Maya Lin's *Vietnam Veterans Memorial*, bring people together, making it possible to speak and act in each other's presence in their differences, as they deal with dilemmas of social life. Such works of art also open the possibility of a more democratic political life, the promise of the radical center.

Beloved is Toni Morrison's masterpiece.[29] It "re-remembers" (the term Morrison introduces in her text) slavery, the task of the main character of the novel and of the novel's readers. The book has been broadly recognized as a, if not the, great American novel, and probably was the major reason why Morrison won the Nobel Prize for Literature. Despite this near-universal praise, a negative review by Stanley Couch reveals how it is that art can play an important role in facilitating remembrance of the barbarism of slavery.

According to Couch, Morrison's writings are saddled by an overly sentimental depiction of African American suffering, drawing from a literary tradition established by James Baldwin, and a stereotypical portrayal of "bestial Black men," influenced by feminist writings of Black women. He concedes that "Morrison, unlike Alice Walker, has real talent, an ability to write a novel in a musical structure, deftly using images as motifs," but he condemns the writing for what he terms "maudlin ideological commercials."[30]

He reviewed the book as if it were a bad TV movie. He summarizes *Beloved* without its musical structure, satirizing it as melodrama. It is a novel about an escaped slave, treated well at first by a benevolent master, but then brutally abused when the master dies, and the cruel overseer takes over. The heroine Sethe escapes pregnant, slave catchers intercede, and she kills her baby in childbirth, instead of condemning her to the life of a slave. Then the long lost father of her children, Paul D., mysteriously returns from the dead and a semblance of a life returns when "beloved," the ghost of the murdered baby, possesses Denver, Sethe's surviving child.

And then Couch offers his satirical acclaim: "Relive some of America's most painful moments—slavery, the Civil War, the efforts made by ex-slaves to experience freedom in a world that was stacked against them from the moment they were sold as work animals. But, most of all, thrill to the love story about the kinds of Americans who struggled to make this country great. (Sethe, Paul D. and Denver walking hand in hand)."

This is like summarizing *Romeo and Juliet* as the story of two mixed-up kids from opposite sides of the tracks who end up killing themselves. Any story can be trivialized by such summary, as it overlooks the artistry, with only banality remaining.

Beloved is formed not as a linear narrative, but a painful circular nightmare, recalled and analyzed. The reader meets characters with uncertainty, not knowing who and what they are, as they only slowly reveal themselves and their relationships. Time and setting are unclear, as are the motivations of the narrated action. The story is told and retold. New details are slowly revealed. Brutalization, powerlessness, and the distortion of normal human relations are given artistic shape. The story is told as it is subjectively remembered in bits and pieces, giving both the reprehensible actions, and their legacies, life.[31]

We observe how under the strain of racism the understanding between Black men and women becomes next to impossible. This is revealed poetically, not polemically, opening up collective memory to include the deeply problematic intersection between race and gender relations in America. And since the distorted relations examined include centrally the relations between a mother and her children, "Beloved" is the ghost of Sethe's murdered child, even more centrally it addresses the additional intersection of generational transference.

Art facilitates memory, which makes possible the constitution of human dignity, despite the most horrific of human experiences: rape and infanticide, as Morrison "re-remembers" the pains and consequences of slavery, giving memory artistic life. The reader explores the difficulty of memory and the unclear problems of responsible actions and their tragedies. Questions are illuminated. The unbearable horror of memory is revealed. Solutions are not presented.

Ida, by Paweł Pawlikowski, illuminates the social condition in a different place and at a different time, concerning different atrocities. But like *Beloved*, the film makes remembering possible. As it focuses on the personal to illuminate the political, it re-remembers.

Ida is a novice, preparing to soon take her vows. Raised as an orphan in the convent, she is informed that she has a living aunt who had chosen to never visit or even reveal herself to Ida. Before taking her vows, her superior instructs Ida that she must try to meet her aunt. Ida did not know of her aunt's existence and only goes on the visit because she is told she must.

The film is about the mysteries between Ida and her aunt, as they are embedded in the Poland of the recent past. It touches troubling issues, the Holocaust and its memory, Polish suffering in and responsibility for those dark times, and Jewish responsibility for Stalinism. All this runs through the specific relationships between Ida and her aunt, and their family and their Polish neighbors.

In its form, as well as its content, the film remembers. Released in 2014, the action takes place in the early 1960s and the dramatic focus is on events that happened during and soon after World War II. It is filmed in black and white, and has the look and feel of films made in the 1960s, comparable to the early films of the great Polish filmmakers of that period, Roman Polanski and Andrzej Wajda.

Indeed, the action moves slowly and at times the beauty of the cinematography resembles exquisite still-life photography, of Polish fields, roads, and thatch-roofed peasant houses, and expressive faces.

The storyline is straightforward, with formal realism, but the images are too exquisite to actually seem real. In the storytelling and the filming an austere minimalism prevails, drawing us back in time. Not surprisingly, given that it covers some very difficult memory problems, *Ida* has been criticized from multiple directions, as anti-Polish and anti-Jewish, as well as for its aesthetic.

The minimalism has been confused with thinness.

The story of a Polish family that saved a Jewish one, until it decided it couldn't any longer, and murdered all but the infant daughter, Ida, has been condemned as anti-Polish.

The portrait of the aunt, as a Jewish anti-Nazi, Communist partisan turned Stalinist prosecutor turned cynic, who drinks too much, sleeps around too freely, and takes full advantage of her privilege, too neatly fits the antisemitic stereotype of *Żydokomuna* (the Jewish Commune).

Critics worry what others might think of the focus on this story and these characters. The film has been condemned because the murdering Polish family is taken to be representative of Poles, the Jewish aunt of Jews. Yet the concreteness of the specific individuals and their stories, and the specific fates of these characters enable the viewer to remember tragic history and illuminate the dimensions of its tragic outcomes. It creates a field of memory, which reveals much that is forgotten in the Polish-Jewish memory conflicts, made possible by the art of the film.

The Vietnam Veterans Memorial was conceived in the then still fresh aftermath of a controversial war. The conception, creation, and ongoing significance of the memorial, as a significant social creation, responds to the social condition as it applies to the memory of a war. It, in fact, has changed the way wars are remembered and has proved to be a model for how societies memorialize and commemorate difficult pasts.

The memorial was built with ambivalence, shared both among the general public and the officials who promoted it. Because of the war's unpopularity, the returning soldiers had not been officially recognized for their service. The memorial was created to right this wrong. The goal was to recognize what distinguished this war from all other American wars—a defeat, broadly unpopular, polarizing the public. But simultaneously to recognize the ways it was similar—primarily there was great sacrifice, with tens of thousands killed and wounded, and many more enduring the war's traumas. Also, as in previous American wars, a significant part of the public understood the war as having been just, supporting it to the end and continuing to support it to this day. The monument embraced and represented the tensions, but at the same time, somehow, has managed to reconcile them, even as they have continued to be present.

The memorial is striking in its simplicity, designed for a specific corner of the National Mall in Washington, composed to the contours of the topography, and its position between the Washington Monument and the Lincoln Memorial, a monument composed of the names of the Americans who died in the war. Lin's minimalism yielded aesthetic and social power to her design. She eloquently illuminated her intentions in creating her masterpiece in an article written soon after the completion of the memorial, but published years after, in 2000.

She underscores her intentions to appeal to a broad spectrum of political opinion: "I wanted to create a memorial that everyone would be able to respond to, regardless of whether one thought our country should or should not have participated in the war."

Wanting the memorial to fit into the contours of the National Mall and its natural beauty and symbolic importance, she worked with the setting not against it: "I had a simple impulse to cut into the earth." And further: "I never looked at the memorial as a wall, an object, but as an edge to the earth, an opened side. The mirrored effect would double the size of the park, creating two worlds, one we are a part of and one we cannot enter. The two walls were positioned so that one pointed to the Lincoln Memorial and the other pointed to the Washington Monument. By linking these two strong symbols for the country, I wanted to create a unity between the nation's past and present."

An element of the design competition was that the monument had to include all the names of the fallen. In Lin's conception: "The need for the names to be on the memorial would become the memorial; there was no need to embellish the design further. The people and their names would allow everyone to respond and remember ... The design is not just a list of the dead. To find one name, chances are you will see the others close by, and you will see yourself reflected through them. I knew the timeline was key to the experience of the memorial: a returning veteran would be able to find his or her time of service when finding a friend's name."

On the overriding importance of the polished black surface: "I always saw the wall as pure surface, an interface between light and dark, where I cut the earth and polished its open edge. The wall dematerializes as a form and allows the names to become the object, a pure and reflective surface that would allow visitors the chance to see themselves with the names. I do not think I thought of the color black as a color, more as the idea of a dark mirror into a shadowed mirrored image of the space, a space we cannot enter and from which the names separate us, an interface between the world of the living and the world of the dead."

And finally she notes her response to the work as a visitor to the memorial: "... the first time I visited the memorial after it was completed I found myself searching out the name of a friend's father and touching it. It was strange to realize that I was another visitor and I was reacting to it as I had designed it."

Memorials as material artifacts work when they are socially received as meaningful by their intended publics. The brilliance of this unconventional memorial is that it understands and cultivates such meaningful social reception, even its creator found herself drawn in. Its aesthetic facilitates a confrontation with the social condition of remembrance of a very difficult war. The great success of Lin's memorial is revealed in the way it has been embraced by a broad public, who continue to remember and forget differently but are able to do so together.

Memory, Art, and the Social Condition

Beloved, Ida, and the Vietnam Veterans Memorial each address a difficult past, which involves memory disputes concerning what is remembered and what is forgotten. These works do not resolve memory conflicts, but they do make it possible to see them in a new light, feel about them differently, embrace alternative points of view, live with and against them in surprising ways. They present a crack in encrusted memories, making it possible to look around and see things differently together, as was Lin's self-conscious intention. It creates a public space for people with conflicting memories to remember together with mutual respect. It is in this sense a radically centrist project.

While not all art accomplishes this and while there are other ways to confront the problems of memory and forgetting, art's critical autonomy, as Adorno illuminated, and its endurance, as Hannah Arendt highlighted, do provide an opening for such accomplishment.

Art demonstrates its autonomy when it follows the logic of its formal invention. This was the central observation of Theodor Adorno and his critical theory colleagues. Art's critical potential is associated with this observation. When the arts develop following their own imperatives, they do so apart from the functionalities of the institutions of systemic social reproduction, both of the state and of the economy; that is, as long as art develops freely, the logic of its development, creation, and appreciation offers an alternative to the logic of capitalism and the state. And as we have seen here, it also offers an alternative to the logic of prevailing and contested collective memories.

To fully appreciate this, it is important to also consider the position of Hannah Arendt that art's endurance through time keeps this alternative open. She offers a different, but complementary perspective on the critical attributes of art and how it can enrich collective memory about difficult pasts. For Arendt, art is non-instrumental work. Its deep cultural significance lies in its immediate uselessness. It's work as an end in itself, creating artifacts in the world beyond utility, tools without specific purpose. Through such work, a world of meaningful artifacts is created. Through such work, when it endures, cultures persist and develop through time. Through such work, a distinctively human world is created.

Exactly what Morrison's critic, Stanley Couch, missed makes it so that *Beloved* does this work and makes an enduring contribution to remembering the difficult past of slavery. It is Morrison's artistry that makes the novel a novel, not a polemic. It illuminates the suffering of slavery and the texture of the suffering, the way it poisoned the relationship between men and women, parents and children. We return to the novel because it is a work of art. It is hard to imagine future novelists not reading and responding to the work, future readers of literature ignoring it. Although we may be mistaken in this, it is the accomplishment of the writing, how it responded to novels past (ironically Couch noticed this as well) and will serve as an inspiration or a foil for novels future. It creates a part of our cultural world that is not defined by political or economic imperatives, and also, crucially for us here, beyond the clichés of one-dimensional collective memory.

Ida also opens memory through art. The film's beauty, the poignancy of the drama between Ida and her aunt, the sympathetic complex ways the Polish family accounts for its treatment of Ida and her family, the equally complex and sympathetic ways Ida's aunt's Communist conviction and dis-illusionment are portrayed, ending with her suicide, Ida's apparent turn from her upbringing and Catholic belief, and her return to the church, all filmed in rich shades of gray, makes for a great film, very much in the tradition of classic films past, Polish, Central European and beyond. It challenges memory clichés of the Polish patriot and anti-antisemite, suggesting alternatives. In this film the beauty of the gray is directly presented.

And the Vietnam Veterans Memorial is a response to memorials past and has fundamentally challenged the memo-rial as a human artifact. Its formal innovations and excel-lence, responding to the demands of conflicting memories, the physical and symbolic environment in which it is located, and the artistic and architectural formal traditions, makes it one of the great public art works of the twentieth century. And this is revealed in the work itself for the professional critics and the judges that originally awarded Lin with the commis-sion. But even more significantly, it becomes clear by the way the work continues to attract visitors, how they use it, with tens of thousands of people leaving meaningful objects to mark the name of a loved one or to just pay respect (all of which have been collected and are now housed in a special warehouse).

Notably, the visitors to the memorial site visit the wall in silence or speak in hush tones, while they speak more loudly and more openly pose for photos and take selfies in the part of the site made up of the more conventional sculpture and the American flag. Lin's work has become a sacred space for people to remember together differently, about a difficult past. This could only be accomplished through a work of art.

Yet, I admit, that now, in the age of Trump in the United States, and Kaczynski in Poland, and Netanyahu in Israel, among many other quasi and not so quasi tyrants, in many other places, with threats to liberal democracy escalating, I wonder whether the subtle rendering of memory of difficult pasts, can withstand memory dogmas, as they legitimate new forms of authoritarianism.

In Poland, it became a matter of official policy that those who explore the tragedies of Polish antisemitism defame the nation. In the United States, the free media have been understood by our highest officials as enemies of the people, and clearly academics are the enemies' fellow travelers, at best.

This obviously requires clear and direct political responses. Demonstrate, write to your representatives, join and support a political party or a social movement, resist, organize. Artistic response, or more precisely art's standing in this, is less instrumental, less partisan, less tendentious. It is ambiguous but, perhaps, just as important, in my judgment, it is enduring.

In this lecture, I have highlighted how art informs memory, and suggested that it can and has supported more inclusive, deliberate, and informed democratic practices, democratic politics of the radical center, in fact. Now things are different:

facing repression, art doesn't form, but defies politics. Or at least it should, if it is not to be barbaric.

Not so far from here, on the National Mall in Washington, there is a slash in the ground and a list of names that questions the dangerous simplicities of jingoistic nationalism, as it is an expression of a regressive patriotism.

Ida examines a tragedy of Polish-Jewish relations, apart from xenophobic politics and the memory practices that justify them, while the ruling party in Poland worked to purge Polish cultural life of "anti-Polish elements," including, tragically, the director of the Polish Cultural Institute in Berlin for presenting "too much Jewish-themed content," i.e., the filming of *Ida*.

Beloved poetically reveals the dilemmas of remembering, with shame and rebellion, the complex legacies of slavery, as Donald Trump, the "Barbarian in Chief" has proclaimed he is "the least antisemitic person you've ever seen in your entire life" and "the least racist person."

Art stands against barbarism, but the continuity of barbaric elements of culture, of the arts, of poetry, broadly understood, persists. We live in a time of political polarization and action imperatives. Art, as it constitutes memory and supports critical reflection on the social condition, turns on a light against the political and cultural blindness characteristic of dark times.

Yet the darkness is descending, Adorno's fear, which I share.

P.S.

The lecture upon which this chapter is based was presented during the first term of Donald Trump's presidency. The chapter is being written as he has been re-elected. I see an ongoing battle between the wisdom and sensibility that poetry and art can cultivate on the one hand, and the barbarism of Auschwitz and those who pursue this path. The battle is ongoing, addressed in the concluding chapters, but it is not just black and white, between the forces of good and of evil. It is as well, and perhaps more significantly, against simplification, cliché, and canned thought, informed by an understanding of the beauty of the gray that can be most movingly portrayed in works of art such as *Beloved*, *Ida*, and the Vietnam Veterans Memorial.

6. Teaching in Afghanistan: Acting as If We Live in a Free Society

At the height of the COVID-19 pandemic, I stepped down from my tenured position at the New School for Social Research. It was voluntary, a redirection, not a resignation. There is no mandatory retirement age in the United States. There were no signs indicating that my work at the New School was unappreciated, and I continued to find it gratifying. Nonetheless, I stuck to a long-term plan to retire at seventy, a plan first imagined when I listened to an extraordinary lecture "The Burden and Blessing of Mortality," by Hans Jonas, published soon after in 1992.

After I stepped down in July 2021, I found myself making an unexpected turn. I had planned to continue my work on the Democracy Seminar, *perhaps teach a course or two each year at the New School, and I started working on a long germinating book, this book. In August, I organized two* Democracy Seminar *webinars with the leadership and professors at the American University of Afghanistan (AUAF), just before and just after the Talban seized power on the 15th. I didn't know it at the time, but these sessions led me down an unforeseen path.*

Following the discussions, I was invited to teach a course on the politics of small things at AUAF, which eventually led to an appointment as a university professor there. I taught online courses on civic engagement, democracy, and the politics of small things. The ideas we are investigating in this book have been central to the courses, gray is beautiful (which burns bright in that context) and the radical commitment to a free public life. I have been actively taking part and contributing to the academic life of the university: not only teaching my classes, but also working with colleagues to add a civic engagement dimension to its programs and classes, and linking our work with universities around the world, especially those that function under repressive conditions.[32] I have also given several public lectures to the university community.

In this chapter, I explain how I came to work at AUAF and how the work revolves around the beauty of the gray. The chapter builds upon a diary I kept as I began this work, and upon one of the lectures I gave at the university.

The Story of My Involvement

As the tide of the war in Afghanistan was turning decisively in the Taliban's favor, my friend and colleague, a past president of the New School for Social Research, Jonathan Fanton, introduced me to Ian Bickford, the president of the American University in Afghanistan. Given my endeavors with Jonathan in the past, including working with the underground democratic opposition in East Central Europe before the transformations of 1989, and fostering regional and then transregional discussions and collaboration on the topic of democracy after 1989, as well as our working together on the liberal arts at the New School (I was briefly his Associate Provost for the Liberal Arts), Jonathan thought that Ian and I should meet. As the Americans troops disengaged, I engaged.

Ian and I met first through Zoom, he in his office in Kabul and I sitting in my study at home in New York, a few weeks before the sweep of the Taliban forces into Kabul. They were then accumulating victories throughout the countryside, circling in on the cities, including Kabul. I remember my astonishment at Ian's calm. He was in the eye of a political hurricane, with chaos surrounding him. I was also struck by his commitment to the university's students and professors, and by his deep appreciation of the mission of the university and to liberal arts ideals. I recognized that he was committed to ideals that were my own and was deeply impressed by how he was acting upon them in extraordinary dangerous circumstances.

Yet, he assured me that he and his colleagues were safe, which as it turns out was not accurate.

We arranged a meeting between several professors at the university and participants of the *Democracy Seminar*, which sponsored the webinar "What the Media Is Not Yelling You About the Situation in Afghanistan." A few weeks later the group had a follow-up webinar on the immediate aftermath of the Taliban victory.

Both webinars were informative. In retrospect, the group seemed to have been less insightful about the balances of forces on the ground, more insightful about the variety and qualities of the forces. Although, along with many other observers, they didn't anticipate the rapid fall of Kabul, the faculty and staff knew who the key players were in their complexity. My colleagues reported on the possible support of the Afghan army by local militias. They knew about and represented the range of political opinions in the cities and the countryside. They talked about the enduring changes in Afghan society over the last twenty years, centering on the impact of education far and wide. They disagreed about how to respond to the Taliban, and their positions on Afghan society and its history were different. I had a hard time, and still am having a hard time, discerning where they stand on the Afghan political map, probably because they have no single stance, apart from their opposition to the present regime, and even that, they articulate differently.

After the Taliban victory, many of the AUAF faculty and staff, along with their students, sought emergency evacuation at the airport. Many of the students were tragically turned back by the American authorities. The faculty and students are now dispersed. The administration and some faculty and students are now based in Doha, Qatar. Faculty and groups of students are also in Iraq, Kyrgyzstan, and just north of my home in the Hudson Valley of New York state, at Bard College, others are scattered around the globe. Notably, after the changes, enrollments are booming with new students in Afghanistan, the majority of them women, taking part in our online courses.

The Fall Semester, 2022

My first semester was winding down. I had been teaching one course, "Civic Engagement and the Politics of Small Things." I was invited to develop the course suggesting how my research and writing on the politics of small things might be applied to an Afghan context. I co-taught the course with colleagues of a broad range of experiences and insights: Nadeem Nooristani, the chair of the Politics and Public Administration Department, Shoaib Rahim, the coordinator of the course, Muska Dastageer, a political scientist who was teaching courses on peace and security, international relations, and conflict resolutions, and Obaidullah Baheer, a lecturer on transitional justice and international relations. They maintain competing judgments about the recent past and the possible future of Afghanistan. They have different ties to the fallen republic, and to the Taliban. Obaidullah was raised and educated as a Salafist, his grandfather, Gulbuddin Hekmatyar is a former mujahideen fighter and Islamist leader, once nicknamed the "Butcher of Kabul." His father was jailed for six years at a CIA torture site, as well as at the Bagram Air Base. Shoaib was part of the Afghan government's team negotiating with the Taliban in Doha, Qatar, and he was also briefly mayor of Kabul. Muska was raised and educated in Denmark, returned to Afghanistan where she was a highly visible critic of government corruption. Nadeem was a translator for many Western press outlets and eventually a CEO of a security agency before joining AUAF as a lecturer in politics and administration before the fall of Kabul. They agree that armed resistance to the Taliban is doomed to failure now, but have different ideas about how to proceed, and what is and what is not possible.

Their respect for each other, despite their differences, is striking, as is their ability to discuss the challenges of civic engagement apart from their competing political positions and experiences. I was reminded of the time, around 2005, when I was exploring with a group of Palestinians and Israelis the possibility of studying and nurturing "the politics of small things" in Israel-Palestine, as described in chapter 4. Then we were interested in illuminating alternatives to repeated brutal wars and terrorism, alternatives to occupation and repression. Among the group were leftist Zionists, post-Zionists and radical anti-Zionists, those who supported a two-state solution and those who insisted on a single secular bi-national state, those who recognized the legitimacy of Israel as a Jewish homeland, and those who categorically opposed the notion. Yet, when we explored the topic at hand, none of this came up. Examining the details of small alternatives to the prevailing regime suspended the need to agree on such issues. It's intriguing to me how this experience was being repeated in my AUAF class. Focusing on lived experience opens up the possibility of freer public discussion. It has a gray political aesthetic. It confronts the complexities of the social condition.

In the class, fighting against despair, we sought under-standing apart from competing grand strategies of liberation. There is a consensus among my colleagues on opposition to the Taliban as it is now ruling Afghanistan, as there was con-sensus among the Palestinian and Israeli scholars examining the abhorrent nature of Israeli occupation and domination of Palestine, but beyond the minimal consensus, their disagree-ment on the optimal political stance toward the Taliban has not come up. Of course, this may not be as significant as I am noting. The planned curriculum determines our focus. Understanding the readings and my lectures is the task at hand. The primary goal of the course is to provide the students with grounds for hope, showing how they can consequentially act, both for themselves, their immediate social circles, and for wider social and political circles, i.e., their country.

As I planned the course, I wanted to introduce the students to the thinkers and political actors who led me to develop my ideas about civic engagement. I developed a syllabus draw-ing upon my "teachers," including Václav Havel and Adam Michnik, Erving Goffman and Hannah Arendt, as well as key works in the sociologies of Max Weber, Emile Durkheim, Georg Simmel, and Jürgen Habermas. I wanted to show the students how their works inform my understanding of the politics of small things, and how this understanding illuminates possible courses of action for the students.

The class opened with excitement. I tried to summarize the project of the course. I explained how we will end by addressing the question: what is to be done? I hoped to pro-vide students with an understanding that even within their very difficult circumstances, in exile or in the country, they can act effectively. I had a four-step plan: to take the students and the faculty through an investigation of the cultural sup-port for such action, "the relative autonomy of culture," to illuminate the domain in which such action takes place, "publics," and the kind of power the action can generate, "politics as concerted action," leading to a consideration of the roles they can play in Afghan society as emerging democratic intellectuals. We would move from 1. cultural freedom, to 2. publics, to 3. concerted action conceptualized as the politics of small things, and then to 4. focus on the role of the intellectual in democratic society, addressing the question "what is to be done?". The syllabus and the weekly assignments were arranged accordingly.

On Cultural Freedom: I presented a sociological approach to cultural freedom. In my account, it exists as artists and scientists get on with their cultural vocations, sustaining ongoing conversations with their predecessors and contemporaries, keeping alive cultural traditions. Cultural creativity and practices have their own logic and trajectories. A practice is free if these trajectories persist despite inevitable political and economic constraints, and if the makers of culture reach their relevant audiences.[33] Such practice provides the opportunity for a public life (as we observed in chapter 5).

Free Public Life: A relatively independent public life is crucial for the alternatives to the prevailing order of things, whether they be democratic or autocratic. I introduced to the students the approaches to the public of Jürgen Habermas, Hannah Arendt, and Erving Goffman, and the way each shows how the creation of social space apart from the command is constituted, and analyzes the cultural and political implications of such social space. Through Habermas, we considered how the creation of a public sphere in relationship to the state and the economy is a constituent element of modern societies. With Arendt, we examined the public domain as the realm of freedom in contrast to the private as the domain of necessity. In Goffman, we explored public space as that of social interaction through which the self and social reality is defined.

The Power of the Politics of Small Things: When people freely meet as equals, in their differences, speak and act in each other's presence and develop a capacity to act in concert, and act upon this capacity, they create power as an alternative to the power of coercion. Drawing on the sociology of Erving Goffman and the political theory of Hannah Arendt, I have tried to demonstrate, how this power has been significant in the politics of East Central Europe. It led to the development of *Solidarność* in Poland and was a significant force that contributed to the fall of previously existing socialism in the Soviet Union and around the Soviet bloc (as we have observed above). This power also has played a significant role in the social movement and electoral politics of the United States, from the civil rights movement to the election of the first African American president of the United States. I shared with the students my understanding and analysis of these historical experiences, and they considered whether they can inform them in considering the challenges they face in their personal and public life. I've been amazed how resonant these ideas have been for my co-teachers and our students. Their excitement charged our examination of the role of intellectuals in democratic society.

Intellectuals: "The intellectuals are special kinds of strangers, who pay special attention to their critical faculties, who act autonomously of the centers of power and address a general public, playing the specialized role in democratic societies of fostering informed discussion about pressing societal issues." I come to this definition in the conclusion of the chapter of

Civility and Subversion entitled "Who are the Intellectuals?". In the course, I unpacked this answer, explaining how its potential significance for them builds upon our inquiry into cultural freedom, publics, and power as concerted action. I wanted to show them how and why they can be intellectuals supporting democracy. How in small ways they can help constitute democratic society, writ large and writ small, as they draw upon their studies to make a difference in their social world.

In addition to teaching the students, I have been mentoring faculty and joined in the university's intellectual community. I have consulted week after week with my co-teachers, and I have given a number of presentations to and participated in university seminars. I produced with colleagues at the university and beyond video-recorded dialogues of the classes. The themes of this book have been the themes of my teaching.

In turn, my colleagues and our students have taught me a great deal about their corner of the world, and how my world looks to them. I saw them facing challenges and dilemmas that are familiar to me, but with notable variations on the familiar themes. They highlight the beauty of the gray, the importance of a principled center, and the need to confront the social condition.

Gray is Beautiful: Michnik wrote about the beauty of the gray, focusing on the politics of moving from an ideology centered party state and society to a liberal democracy. I have shifted the focus, applying the sensibility of life in an ongoing, but flawed liberal democracy. My Afghan colleagues and students, and I thinking along with them, have shifted the focus once again, realizing the importance of the sensibility in the aftermath of a failed and flawed liberal democratic project, the Afghan Islamic Republic, in the face of a theo-cratic autocracy, the Taliban regime.

They are in an apparently hopeless situation, rejecting the new regime, but quite uncertain about how to proceed. They oppose the Taliban, but the ways and the reasons they oppose it are quite different. A few apparently can't completely rule out armed resistance, though almost all of them, as far as I can discern, do. Too much suffering in armed resistance and from civil war are fresh memories. Others believe that nonviolent resistance is the only way, while others see it as futile. Still others believe that there is no alternative but to attempt to move the regime in a positive direction, seeking a more liberal Taliban faction, seeking some form of positive collaboration, working to deliver scarce goods—food, medicine, shelter, and education—to the downtrodden. But others view all or most of such activities as collaboration in the most negative sense, seeing it as fortifying and legitimating the reprehen-sible regime.[34] There is a temptation to see their competing judgments in stark black and white terms, most apparent on "Afghan Twitter," where factional denunciation is the favored mode of expression. And this factionalism is radicalized by ethnic suspicions and tensions, among Pashtun, Tajik, and Hazara, and others, with competing narratives of self and other, and significant linguistic differences. But despite all this, in a way because of it, my colleagues recognize that there is a pressing necessity that they together recognize that things are not clear. It is a matter of grays. While working with the Taliban is distasteful, working to feed the hungry, provide healthcare for the ailing, and working to educate the younger generation, especially the girls and young women under the yoke of gender apartheid, is a necessity.

My students and colleagues are uncertain. The more secu-lar and the more religiously observant, as they are, don't know what is the best way to proceed. They are aware of the distance between themselves, part of the urban educated elite, and their more traditional compatriots in the countryside (for some, their families back home). They themselves are ambivalent about the Western-supported-and-imposed twenty years of the Islamic Republic. For many, its failure proves that democracy is not for them or at least that Afghanistan is not ready for democracy. But on the other hand, the Taliban theocracy is repellent. Should the goal be a "true," more tolerant, Islamic governance or is it a matter of getting democracy right? Perhaps the problem is the very notion of Afghanistan as a nation-state? I've heard many interesting ideas from committed Islamists to committed liberal democrats, from those who lean on what they have learned from the liberal tradition, and those who lean on radical criticisms of that tradition.

But among them all, I observe a commitment to the better and not to the perfect, an appreciation that gray is beautiful and that among themselves they need to pursue an acceptable range of gray shades.

The Radical Center

They recognize a need for public deliberation among those who oppose the Taliban order. But they are fully aware of the difficulties in initiating and sustaining such deliberation.

As my colleague, Muska Dastageer has written:

> As a commentator of Afghan politics, what I discern is that
> ... fragmentation has led to a situation where the very foundations of conversation are destabilized. In clarifying your premises, before outlining the argument itself, conversation is often rendered impossible. Before even speaking, an identitarian focus has made the fixities of identity the entry points

for conversation. Even the adjective "Afghan" is disputed, with some currents in discourse ... arguing that it is synonymous with one ethnic group, the Pashtuns .... More and more, determination of ethnic identity is a qualifier for the merit of your argument. That is, it is no longer the substance of your argument which matters for the adjudication of its merit. It is as much who makes it, and not by virtue of past speech or actions, but by virtue of immutable characteristics.

As a result:

... no Archimedean point for dialogic engagement exists anymore among different political or ethnic Afghan groupings. It is no longer possible to trace back from the incongruent positions in political discourse to points opponents can agree to. The reason likely lies in the precedent-dissolving, conflagration-like nature of the republic's collapse. In the historical sweep of the past five decades, it came as a conclusion to the project of progressivism. Another failed experiment of governance. In that conflagration, it has seemed that outlooks for different options have come to seem achievable, "real," where they seemed unachievable, "unreal," before. Philosopher of ethics, Bernard Williams, notes that a real option for a group is an outlook they already inhabit *or one they could go over to in their actual historical circumstances.*[35]

Afghans can't find a common ground that provides for them a means to disagree with mutual respect, so that they can listen to each other, consider their alternative perspectives and opposing observations and judgments. Dastageer's fear is that in this public vacuum, autocracy can prevail without significant opposition. She and her colleagues, thus, when looking at the prospects for her native land, are tempted to despair.

Here the primary importance of the commitment to a free public life is most apparent, proof of the radical commitment to a center where differences can be considered, not only for the society, the nation-state at large, but also at the margins, in miniature, in the realm of the politics of small things. On this, they agree. The absence of a viable free public life has stimulated a radical commitment to such life.

The Social Condition

They know that their need to talk to each other with mutual respect, despite their differences of opinion, regional, ethnic, and linguistic differences, and various commitments to Islam and secularism, is more important than their differences. But doing this, even in the university, is difficult. Not only are their differences and conflicting commitments always in the background; there is also a tension between the pedagogic responsibilities of the university and its public responsibilities.

I observed this as I was teaching. In the second session of my teaching, I was presenting an overview of a fundamental finding of sociology: with the development of modern complex societies, the institutions and practices of religion, economics, politics, and culture separate from each other. Economic activity becomes less circumscribed by the organized religion, the state, and cultural traditions and practices. The state is more independent from religious institutions, as are the arts and sciences, and vice versa. All the founders of modern social science start with this observation, with important variations on this theme. I explain how this is the observation of such towering figures as Karl Marx, Max Weber, Ferdinand Tönnies, Emile Durkheim, and Georg Simmel, among many others. I presented this overview, drawing on my work published in *On Cultural Freedom*, because it lays the groundwork for understanding the importance of cultural freedom as a basis for significant alternative action in repressive contexts. It's an important first step of our investigation that provides for them an understanding of the possibilities open to them for becoming civically engaged even given the atrocious conditions under which they live. To get the full benefit of the class, they need to understand this first move. But the move provoked them to start a discussion on the chat function of the Zoom meeting. They debated among themselves to what degree such theories, developed in Western, Christian societies, apply to theirs, to a Muslim society, to Afghanistan. They debated whether such separation between religion and politics was possible in the Afghan countryside, even if it did apply to life in the capital and the major cities of Afghanistan, and they debated whether such separation is a good thing. After the session was over, I asked my colleagues to provide the transcript of the discussion and found it fascinating. My co-teachers, though, were concerned. Having such debate was all well and good, but they were worried that the students weren't paying sufficient attention to the lesson of the lecture.

We faced a dilemma, especially ironic in a class on civic engagement and the politics of small things. Focusing on pedagogy can get in the way of a rare opportunity for the students to engage in public dialogue, while supporting a rare moment of open political exchange can get in the way of crucial teaching and learning.

We saw two ways of dealing with this dilemma. Holding university events on such topics and collaborating with groups beyond the university to create a forum for such discussion. An example of the former is the "Rule of Law" series sponsored by the Law Department at the university. The lecture I gave to the series is an example, discussed below. A significant next step would be to constitute similar series beyond the university, connecting with students and colleagues both in Afghanistan and the diaspora to discuss the pressing issues that they face.

Universal Human Rights "As If"

I had an opportunity to help take the first step soon after I joined the faculty. Haroun Rahimi, the chair of the university's Law Department, asked me to contribute to the Department's "Rule of Law" lecture series. I had first met Haroun at the initial webinars I organized between the university and *Democracy Seminar*. We have co-taught a course entitled "Thinking About Democracy." I welcomed and was honored by his invitation, but was, at first, unsure about how I could contribute to the series. Although I was pleased and honored to be asked, I must admit, I was also surprised and challenged.

My surprise had to do with the theme of the series, "The Rule of Law." The challenge was for me to say something intelligent about it. I am not a lawyer or a student of the law. I am very much in favor of the rule of law. I know that people who live in countries where it is normative, where it is alive as an ideal, even if not always enacted in practice, are better off than those who don't live under these conditions. I know I have been very fortunate that I have lived in such a society, though I fear that this may not be the case in the future given recent developments in the United States (analyzed below in the concluding chapters). I know in my personal experience people who don't live under the rule of law and therefore have suffered, among them many of my colleagues, students, friends, and even a relative, from around the world, from Iran to Argentina, from Myanmar to Romania to China (where my son's wife was born), and of course now, in Afghanistan.

But I haven't studied the rule of law. So, I hesitated when Haroun Rahimi asked me to contribute to this series. I wanted to contribute but wasn't sure how I could. I thought that perhaps through a careful conversation between the two of us, we together could identify what I might be able to say that would be of interest. We talked and came up with the topic, "human rights and the rule of law." I understood the presentation as a continuation of the conversation that Haroun and I started.

As we discussed the issue of human rights, I realized that while I don't have any special expertise in the rule of law as such, I could say something about its social interactive infrastructure, about how the rule of law is sustained in social orders in which it formally exists and how it is pursued in social orders in which it most assuredly does not officially exist. The discussion pointed to remarks in grays, not "human rights under a rule of law, or no human rights," but how the ideals of human rights under the rule of law is practically achieved through social interaction in repressive, as well as more open societies.

I started by presenting my key thesis: when people act as if they are free, even in the most repressive of circumstances, they are, consequently, free, as long as they can sustain their actions, though this may be quite difficult. To confirm this thesis, I built upon my observations of the struggles for democracy, human rights, and human dignity under the shadows of Communist oppression in East Central Europe and then turned to an analysis of grounds for universal human rights. I presented an alternative to, or at least supplement to, idealistic philosophical and religious grounding of the universality of rights, and sought to show the limitations of the realistic, skeptical critiques of universality based on the proposition that it is only states that can guarantee rights. I tried to demonstrate that rights are socially constituted apart from the power of the state and that this has pressing relevance for the AUAF community, the people of Afghanistan, and far beyond.

To be clear, I was not arguing that states, both nation-states and international agreements among them, don't matter when it comes to human rights. I know, quite the contrary, that nation-states and international organizations and agreements clearly are of the utmost importance, from bills of rights to international pacts of human rights. But for them to be consequential, I wanted to underscore, they must be acted upon in daily practice, where state supports exist, as well as in societies where human rights are denied as a matter of state policy. In such societies, the preconditions for human rights can be created in daily practices, anticipating fundamental changes, but even more than this, also immediately constituting them apart from the repressive regime.

This assertion is based upon a key sociological theorem, usually called the Thomas theorem, named after the early twentieth-century sociologist, W. I. Thomas, but actually it was not only his insight, but also that of his wife, Dorothy Swaine Thomas. "If men define situations as real, they are real in their consequences."

A side irony: obviously the sexism of the time, the 1920s, the word "men" here purportedly includes both men and women. Not so obvious and tragic, for much of the last century W. I. was credited with this theorem, while Dorothy Swaine was dropped. When, in fact, the formulation first appeared in their co-authored book *The Child in America*. This irony actually illuminates my topic. Because Dorothy Swaine's contribution to the social sciences was ignored, it was confirmed that social science was a man's domain. And as a consequence, their academic home, the university, was a man's domain.

And in terms of my education at the University of Chicago, the contributions to the Chicago school of sociology included W. I. Thomas, George Herbert Mead, and Robert E. Parks, but not Dorothy Swaine Thomas and Jane Addams (known as a distinguished social reformer, but not as the sociologist that she was).

Returning to the question of human rights and the rule of law and my provocation that they can be grounded beyond states or notions of natural law: without knowing anything about the Thomas theorem, a fundamental insight of the democratic opposition in East Central Europe in the late 1970s and 1980s was the irony that zones of freedom could and should be constituted by acting as if they lived in a free society. They acted as if they lived in a free society and because they acted in this way and weren't thoroughly repressed, they created zones of freedom, even the institutions of a free society.

A whole alternative system of public life, a public sphere as Jürgen Habermas imagined it, was created, starting with the publication of alternative sources of news and analysis, and a range of cultural expression that would have been censored in official publishing.

The first publication was an information bulletin with news about the repressive actions of the party state and the responses by the then small democratic opposition. When I read, in my AUAF email box, Asadullah Chakary's ground reports, I am reminded of the *Bulletin of Information* publications in the late 1970s in Poland.[36]

Step by step, year after year, in the 1970s and 1980s, a complete publication system and public domain apart from the official one was created. Following the publication of the *Bulletin of Information*, a series of literary, artistic, and political magazines were published. Independent poetry readings were conducted, music and theater performances and discussion

groups were developed in private apartments and other un-
likely public spaces, such as in church basements and annexes,
and on the streets and outside of apartment complexes. There
was even clandestine hacking of state television broadcasts,
the organizers of which at one point helped me attend a trial
of Adam Michnik.

At this point, I must point out how startling all this was at
the time. Under Communist control and direction, with totalitarian ambitions, all life was under the control of the Party.
Nothing happened on the streets, in museums, libraries,
theaters, schools, universities, stores, and factories that wasn't
monitored and controlled by the Party. All publications were
censored, as were a broad range of the arts and sciences.

In this setting, an alternative academic movement was
constituted, "The Flying University." Such activity anticipated
and then supported, the development of a well-coordinated
labor movement, *Solidarność*, formally "The Independent Self-
Governing Trade Union Solidarity," the cumbersome name the
result of contestation and compromise among its members.

Freedom of speech and expression were asserted, as was
freedom of assembly. And they were justified by referring to
the Helsinki Accords, signed in 1975, that legitimated the geopolitical status quo of post war, a victory for the ruling powers
of the Soviet bloc, but also committed to human rights which
led to Helsinki Watch and Human Rights Watch and other
civic institutions that monitored the struggle for human rights
internationally. Significantly, this monitoring came to include
oppositional activity all around the former Soviet bloc.

Acting as if one lived in a free society was supported by an
international agreement among states. Something that was notably present in Czechoslovakia, where Charter 77 was the main
oppositional force, as it echoed the international agreements.
But it also worked the other way around. An international

agreement among states was consequential because people acted as if they lived in a free society. It was not only the right of individuals of conscience to speak their truth. It was a matter of individuals together acting to support such speech and for such speech to circulate. This included prominent, creative, and brave individuals, such as Adam Michnik and Václav Havel who were heroes of the democratic opposition, authors of the classic essays of opposition political culture, respectively "The New Evolutionism" and "The Power of the Powerless," which we read in my civic engagement class at AUAF (and will be explored more fully in chapter 8). But from the point of view of considering the social constitution of human rights, it included thousands of others who managed to edit, publish, print, and distribute their writing, along with all those who read them in unofficial publications. They bought and borrowed the readings in their circle of acquaintances and friends and discussed them, in alternative public spaces, including as I argued in the opening of my book, *The Politics of Small Things*, in the most private of places, around kitchen tables.

A rich-textured fabric of social interactions, thus, was constituted, supporting the freedom of expression and association.

In some ways in our present digital age, things are easier now. Dozens of people had to work together to compile and distribute *The Bulletin of Information*. Now, I imagine, Asadullah Chakary, the AUAF security reporter, gets his information from a circle of friends, acquaintances, and sources, writes it up, sends out email bulletins, and we receive them and perhaps share them. We can easily then debate the news from this source and the many sources of the global media, offering interpretations and opinions, laud those with whom we agree, criticize those with whom we disagree on social media. Alternative forms of public opinion develop, with alternative shared common sense.

When I lived in Poland in the 1970s, I would wait in line for an hour to get my hands on the *International Herald Tribune* and I would search the shortwave radio dial with great care to listen to Radio Free Europe, Voice of America, and the BBC, to gain access to news about the world and about Poland. Now it takes incredible efforts on the part of repressive states to block such access. In many places, the capacity of ordinary people to access forbidden news and information appears to be greater than the capacity of repressive authorities to block access, as it would appear to be the case with the Taliban in Afghanistan.

The ease is, though, perhaps not only a gift, but also a problem. Because of the difficulty in constituting the alternatives, they persisted. Specific relationships of trust and mutual interdependence were created. Now mediated connections can easily be formed, but also can be easily turned off. But note, that when the interaction has institutional support, such as that which it gets at AUAF, it is, can, and has been sustained, with high quality.

I have been heartened when I hear reports coming out of Afghanistan that improvised online education is being conducted for young women and girls inside the country. They are acting as if they live in a society free of gender discrimination, indeed, gender apartheid. I wonder about what kind of institutional support they are getting, what kind of institutional support can be developed by and for them.

This suggests, I believe, ways that we can make it more likely that the "acting as if" can indeed become a reality. Doing so would make it so that the human rights of the freedom of speech and expression and of association would be enacted, and if the focus is on hunger or gender equality, or inter-ethnic respect and equality, the rights associated with these goals would also be supported.

If civic associations and institutions such as AUAF act as if gender equality and the freedoms associated with it are real, at least for those inside the community, they are real as a consequence. And if we are observed and we intentionally show these principles to those outside our community, we create for them gender equality and freedoms as a norm that they can potentially work to adopt. Performing human rights in everyday life constitutes those rights as real in its consequences.

When Haroun and I decided on the topic of my lecture, I was recalling Arendt's critical response to the powerlessness of human rights talk when it came to horrors of the modern barbarism of the twentieth century. Despite the declarations of universal human rights, those who didn't live within polities that defended those rights, had none. She knew this as a matter of personal experience having lived for years as a Jewish refugee fleeing Nazi Germany. And she noted, as I recognize some who watched my lecture know from their experiences, the tenuousness of the rights of stateless refugees.

I followed her insight in my lecture but made an important amendment. I highlighted that her observation should be qualified because of the political power of the definition of the situation, making my point by recalling the experience of the opposition movement in East Central Europe. The citizen rights that she highlighted can be the rights of people who interact with each other apart from states that support the rule of law. Human rights are citizen rights, but the citizenship is not an exclusive matter of official policies of nation-states. It includes rights constituted in social interactions pitted against states, with the definition of the situation playing a key role. The universality of human rights applies to any one circumstance if people act together as if it were so. With this conclusion, I can draw two key implications.

In nation-states where recognition of human rights is part of a codified rule of law, either explicitly as in the United States constitution, or implicitly as in the United Kingdom without a written constitution, human rights depend on social interactions where people critically confirm that they are enacting the principle both in the simple application of the law and in the critical evaluation of the law's limits, then highlighting the shortcomings of official claims, working to make purported ideals a component of a lived reality. This requires the work in my country, for example, of civil rights movements: African American, feminist, LGBTQ+, and that of the Indigenous, along with lawyers and judges and the courts. Thurgood Marshall, both as a great civil rights advocate and as Supreme Court justice, personified my argument. This work is especially significant now, with the retreat of democracy in the United States, which we will analyze here in the closing chapters.

On the other hand, in nation-states where human rights are not officially recognized and are officially attacked, such as in Afghanistan today and around the old Soviet bloc in the not-so-distant past, human rights depend on social interaction that critically constitute their universality in opposition to the official order. They crucially depend upon groups of individuals and even institutions that stand apart from officialdom, at least to some degree "acting as if they live in a free society," institutions such as AUAF, and perhaps other institutions of higher education and research in the country, and outside the country in organizations like Human Rights Watch and like Helsinki Watch before it.

I maintained in concluding my remarks to the students and faculty of AUAF that this presents real opportunities for them and for their friends and colleagues elsewhere. I taught the theory behind this lesson to my colleagues and students at the AUAF, as they have been demonstrating to me in their responses in our class sessions and in the lecture, how to put it into practice in their most difficult of circumstances.

7. Tocqueville's *Democracy in America* and Making America Great Again

I first read Alexis de Tocqueville's Democracy in America *as a college freshman. When I embarked on my study of the politics of American culture and the culture of American politics, which eventually led to the publication of my book* The Cynical Society, *I started reading his classic more closely and maturely. Then, and for many years after, I taught a course on Tocqueville's book and his topic at Eugene Lang College, the New School's liberal arts undergraduate college. Most recently, I have been re-reading and thinking about Tocqueville's reflections in dialogue with my colleagues and students at the American University of Afghanistan (AUAF), as they have informed a course I have been coordinating, "Thinking About Democracy." These readings are the grounds for this chapter. An earlier version was delivered as my contribution to a conference at the New School in May 2022, "American Democracy in Crisis." The chapter was completed as my work at AUAF was coming to an end, as my fellow Americans re-elected Donald Trump as president of the United States.*

As a freshman in college, I read *Democracy in America* in a history class, as the book is most often admired and cited. It's intriguing how many of Tocqueville's observations about the strengths and weaknesses of the American political system and social order have endured: the workings of the federal system, the separation of powers, the promise, perils, and consequences of individualism, the potential dangers of the tyranny of the majority, and much more.

Yet, there were also passages I found perplexing, and still do. Tocqueville considered race and racism in America through a racist lens, demonstrated by his approving citation of Thomas Jefferson's theories presented in *Notes on the State of Virginia*. His analyses of gender relations and the powerful character of American (democratic) women were inventive, but so patriarchal that they are difficult to comprehend. And while it is intriguing that he foresaw the likelihood of class conflict in America, in his terms a consequence of "the aristocracy of manufacturers," he saw disaster on the horizon, as was also the case in his view of the races and their prospects, not a promise for social transformation.

On the central problems of race, gender and sexuality, and class, Tocqueville is not the best of guides in considering today's crisis of democracy in America. Frederick Douglas and Ida B. Wells, to say the least, are much better guides.[37] Although he reluctantly was letting go of his class privilege, as he clung to his racial and gender privilege, and this didn't provide insight, I still think that Tocqueville has much to offer in understanding America and the present crisis in our democracy.

He perceived major tensions knitted into the fabric of the political and social order of democracy and the United States. His analysis and judgment about the outcome of these tensions were historically specific. But they do, nonetheless, provide critical insight into the crisis of democracy in America in our times, the starting point of my work *The Cynical Society*. Here, I present an elaboration of that work. I maintained that the cynicism from which American society suffers is in persistent tension with its democratic characteristics, and that ongoing democratic efforts are the answer to the challenges to cynicism.[38] Tocqueville's investigation of the dangers and remedies of the tyranny of the majority illuminates the dangers of a new tyranny of a minority in our times, and his investigation of democratic culture, as the American arts and sciences, explains its populist and anti-intellectual features, suggesting the potential to overcome these features. Moving toward this conclusion, I propose we consider the major themes of volume 1 and volume 2 of *Democracy in America*, informed by an overview of his general sensibility.

Volume 1 and the New Tyranny of the Minority

Tocqueville was profoundly ambivalent about democracy, as I believe is also the case for my Afghan colleagues and students, though for very different reasons. He and they do not take democracy for granted, and because of this, he was able to critically appraise its promise and perils with a perspective different than most of us in the West or whose thoughts have been shaped by Western experience. He was a sophisticated man of his times. This explains the limitations of his accounts of race, class, and gender in America, but it also explains the power of his observations about democracy and its culture.

On the one hand, Tocqueville perceived that democracy was inevitable, an unfolding "providential force," as he put it, that can be shaped for better or for worse, but can't be stopped. On the other hand, he was deeply concerned about cultural judgments and distinctions that democracy overwhelms: the freedoms, the creative accomplishments, the refinement and excellence, the public virtues, the traditions, to which he was attached. My Afghan colleagues echo his concerns: they wonder, are the culture and practices of democracy compatible with the practices and culture of Afghanistan, and if so: are they desirable? I think Tocqueville can be a guide to answering their questions.

He was a nineteenth-century aristocrat who presciently saw an inevitable democratic future that others didn't recognize. But he also was nostalgic for a world passing, in which a timepiece of quality, an object of refined craftsmanship, was replaced by a mass-produced watch, and the columns of fine homes were made of marble and not painted wooden facades, as he observed upon entering New York harbor (examples he cited in the text).

He saw a world emerging, indeed our world, in which democracy is a nearly universally embraced ideal, even by dictators and dictatorships that most often justify their diktats as necessary steps on the road to a mature democracy.

Just a few years before Tocqueville wrote his magnum opus, the founders of the American republic still adhered to the long-established wisdom that democracy is a prelude to tyranny. They were highly suspicious of "the rule of the rabble" and sought to control it, yielding the many undemocratic qualities of the American system.[39] Yet, Tocqueville judged that the experience of America, the way of life that had developed here, could prove to be the exception to this inherited rule. Exploring America, he saw new possibilities.

Tocqueville appreciated the ingenuity of the American experiment. He understood that democracy is not just a system of governance, with strengths and weaknesses, but also understood how this system was built on a social and cultural infrastructure, a product of fortune and design, constituted by social equality and individualism. He illuminated the connection between equality, individualism, and democracy, and the problems these connections posed. His logic: democracy is predicated on equality. Equality fosters individualism, and in turn individualism creates atomization, which opens the door to manipulation. As he traveled around America, he observed the implications of the logic, both positive and negative.

In voluntary associations, "individualism properly understood," a broad-minded enlightened individualism, the separation of powers, federalism, and much else, Tocqueville saw the grounds upon which the ideals of freedom and equality could be balanced. But he saw this as not necessarily a done deal; dynamic tensions were at play.

He presented dramatic accounts of the undersides of democracy, the aspects of democracy that inherited political thought were necessary outcomes of democratic rule: "the tyranny of the majority" and what he explained as "the despotism democracies have to fear most," the despotism that would be later described as the product of mass consumer society. He then shows how American safeguards protect against these undersides.

He thought that American individualism was of a specific variety, in which the calculation of individual interest included consideration of the broader public interest. He understood federalism and the system of checks and balances would temper the concentration of centralized power. He believed that robust civic associations, positioned between a potentially too-powerful state and weak individuals, would protect the citizenry. And he thought that newspapers, we would say news media, robustly developed as they have been in America, would support the development of civil and political associations, and the overall pluralism of the society and the decentralization of power.

Not so long ago, this led some of his prominent concerned followers, "neo- Tocquevillians," from liberal right and left, I'm thinking of three "Roberts": Nisbet, Putnam, and Bellah, to worry about the safeguards, to worry about the decline of organized religion, to worry about "people bowling alone," to worry about the loss of a community.

Yet, although I still perceive these dangers, I believe we're in a radically different situation now. I think that aspects of the very protections against the tyranny of the majority and democratic despotism that Tocqueville detected are supporting a new tyranny, a tyranny of a populist minority.

The tension he perceived in the American political and social order, between popular excesses and stabilizing controls, avoiding tyranny, still are in play. Yet, aristocrat that he was, he didn't anticipate that the controls could lead to the very real prospect of the destruction of democracy in America, empowering a segmented populist control of democracy, rather than the refined tempering of democratic excesses that he supported. To put it bluntly, federalism, checks and balances, the electoral college, and judicial review are now undermining the capacity of the majority to govern wisely.

Through Tocqueville's lens, we can perceive that we're in a crisis, or a series of crises, because the will of the majority cannot prevail on multiple issues of deep and broad public concern. On matters of social and economic justice, addressing the looming environmental catastrophe, gun violence, and our relationships with the rest of the world, we appear to no longer be capable of majority rule.

And when we consider why the majority can't rule, it appears to be lodged in the very institutions and practices that Tocqueville thought would soften democratic excesses. Voluntary associations of a new sort, converted into highly motivated special interest groups, such as the NRA (the National Rifle Association), have dominated policymaking. Federalism has given the citizens of small, rural states, often with political perspectives not responding to the crises of our times, much more power than those from large more urban ones. The judiciary, most dramatically, the Supreme Court, is now assaulting the rights of woman, African Americans, democratic advances in the expansion of full citizenship, the voting rights law, and reproductive rights, as it supports the dominant powers of corporations and the super-rich, and the unitary executive power of the president. And the media regime is radicalizing these minority powers, turning cultural and political pluralism into political tribalism, in which the prospect of a civil war is actively imagined by right-wing populists, inspired and provoked by the current president of the United States.

I draw these concerns primarily from the first volume of *Democracy in America*, which was quite well received by his American contemporaries. Volume 2 was another matter.

Volume 2: The Danger of Democratic Culture

While volume 1 was an appreciation of American political institutions and social arrangements, which I believe now are turning against American democracy, volume 2 is more focused on American, i.e., democratic, culture—what it does well and what it does poorly, and the danger it poses. I am again going to turn Tocqueville on his head, as I think about the present crisis, pointing to the creative promise of democratic culture that Tocqueville did not recognize.

Tocqueville's investigation of the arts and sciences in America is based on his most fundamental proposition: America is a society that is egalitarian. At my first reading, in the late 1960s, this was a proposition that still seemed to make some sense. But since then, it would seem that this is more and more difficult to accept. Rising inequality is a major global problem that is most acute in the United States, with the rich getting ever richer, especially the super-rich, leaving the rest of us in the dust, especially those without higher education or specialized skills.

Yet despite this, as I have introduced Tocqueville to my students, I have long suggested that it doesn't get to a central point: the democratic culture of Americans and the impact this has on American social and political life. I investigated this in *The Cynical Society*, which I explained in its introduction could have been entitled "The Democratic Society," because I believed, following Tocqueville, that cynicism and democracy are two sides of the same coin.

Social mobility, upward and downward, is nothing like what Tocqueville described and most Americans imagine. Realizing the so-called American dream is very far from the lived experience of most Americans. It's ironically more a reality of contemporary Nordic European societies than our own, as a Danish politician once observed in a poignant lecture here at the New School, entitled, "The American Dream Comes to Life in Denmark." Yet, the Americans' "habits of the heart," as Tocqueville put it, are still democratic. I worked to convince my students of this years ago, though I realize my argument is becoming harder to sustain.

The contrast between the lived and imagined reality is perversely expressed in the notion that Donald Trump is a blue-collar billionaire. More seriously, the vast majority of Americans describe themselves as middle class, even though the wage and wealth differences of those who define themselves as such is immense, from those who must work hard to feed, clothe and shelter themselves, to those who do so grandly.

Although we are not, we imagine ourselves as equals and this imagination matters. While an important prospect in our politics is the abandonment of this delusion, revealed in the attitudes of the young toward capitalism and socialism and the appeal of Bernie Sanders and other political candidates of the left, and in the growing resentment of the rural and less educated of the urban and the more educated, egalitarianism is very much still central to America's political culture.

Tocqueville got to the core of this in the opening of volume 2, starting with his most ironic observation:

> America is ... the one country in the world where the precepts of Descartes are least studied and best followed ... Americans do not read Descartes's works because their social state turns them away from speculative studies, and they follow his maxims because the same social state naturally disposes their minds to adopt them.[40]

We assume that we are all equal and that our opinions are equal as well. With this ethos, Americans, as democrats, view inherited and contemporary cultural authority with suspicion. We are radical skeptics. Expert, refined knowledge and insight must prove themselves. Since we are all equal, no person's opinion or judgment is inherently superior to others. And thus, as we are practicing Cartesians, we don't bother to read Descartes, but we practice his radical skepticism.

Tocqueville then goes on to reflect on a broad range of issues: American aptitude and taste for general ideas, the relationship between religion and democracy, the American optimistic ideas about "the indefinite perfectibility of man," the tendency of Americans to practice the sciences rather than to investigate theory, the American spirit of cultivating the arts and literature, and the way American democracy has modified the English language, among many other topics. The American egalitarian ethos explains this all in Tocqueville's account.

Experts in the arts and sciences, including medicine, are viewed with suspicion, especially when their assertions are not immediately apparent, hidden in knowledge about microscopic organisms that are not readily apparent. Established grounds for judgment, legitimized by peer review, degrees, and certificates are not automatically accepted. And since we are all equal, quantity substitutes for quality. The most popular opinion can easily substitute for informed opinion. So-called common sense overrules expertise.

Think about Donald Trump's suggestion that we use a disinfectant spray to combat COVID-19. Think not only of the public's suspicion of public health authorities, but also of legal experts on the workings of the constitution, and the idea that the news sources adhering to established journalistic standards are no better than the blogs, podcasts, and tweets that denounce them. And if everyone you know agrees with you on this or that matter, you know you are right, and "they" are wrong.

In sum, Tocqueville in his analysis of American arts and sciences in the early nineteenth century revealed the way American anti-intellectualism of the twentieth and twenty-first centuries is a basic characteristic of the American way of life. And this, I believe, has empowered looming dangers of the tyranny of a minority that we are now experiencing.

Yet, just as it was the case that the American protections against the tyranny of the majority were not assured in the past, the dangers of the anti-intellectual, the anti-democratic tyranny of the minority is now not a done deal, and I get this from Tocqueville.

His greatest accomplishment, in my judgment, is not that he presciently foresaw the future or that he somehow unlocked the key to the American (democratic) genius, as I was taught as a college freshman. Rather, I believe that he illuminated key tensions in American democratic life: the long-recognized tense relationship between democracy and tyranny, and the more recently recognized tension between democracy and the despotism of an anti-intellectual populist segment of a polarized society. Tocqueville's gift to us is the illumination of tensions inherent to American democracy. Sometimes this led him to mistaken conclusions, such as in his observations about race, class, and gender.

In interesting ways, his conclusions about American democratic culture also were mistaken, but in this case his mistake points to promise instead of unforeseen perils. Thus, he explained why American literature was inferior to British literature exactly when American literary brilliance was emerging, through Emerson, Thoreau, Melville, Dickenson, Whitman, et al. As an aristocrat, as an elitist, he did not understand the power of the words and deeds of commoners, or work that drew upon their experiences. Like Theodor Adorno, the power of jazz would have escaped him. He would not anticipate Hemingway is my guess, and even more so Roth, Ellison, and Morrison. Yet such creativity is the promising result of the tensions he highlighted: refined culture not destroyed by the vernacular but empowered by it.

I think the outcomes of these tensions are revealing new looming dangers, the rise of a tyranny of the minority, empowered by anti-intellectualism. Considering the outcome of the United States presidential election of 2024, I share Tocqueville's concerns and am deeply troubled that a major battleground were interviews on bro and sex positive podcasts to audiences that only know what they know about politics through these forums, along with cable news programs that do little more than confirm the political prejudices of their audiences.

But I also note that there is a strikingly countervailing development, in news, analysis, and interpretation, using a variety of media and cultural forms that broaden perspectives from the refined and previously excluded. It is notable in the United States that women, African Americans, LGBTQ+ people, American Latinos, and Asians are appearing in increasing numbers in art worlds, publishing, newsrooms, in laboratories and art studios, on stage, in film, and on television, transforming our public life and culture. And how new forums that specialize in providing public space for the marginalized are flourishing: online magazines, podcasts, publishing houses, etc. These are now bases for hope. The democratic cultural creativity that Tocqueville missed in nineteenth-century America, has come to define American culture in the twenty-first. The previously marginalized have come to define present-day American culture as Albert Murray explored in considering how the blues and jazz defined it in the early twentieth century. Perhaps this doesn't have immediate broad political effect, but it does penetrate, infect in a way, the broader public. It is a key to public innovation. The general culture is now much more cognizant of the experiences and insights of the previously marginalized. Bi-racial love and marriage are accepted with little hesitation. A broader range of sexual and romantic experiences are now routinely positively expressed in writing, film, and television, as are the experiences and views of Asian Americans, the Indigenous, and religious minorities with the diminishing dominance of Christians in America. This is a great democratic achievement for many.

But for others it is a looming disaster. There is the reactionary response from others, those who would like to turn back the clock, who would like "to make America great again." MAGAism, I believe, should be understood in this way. The American presidential election of 2024 as well as of 2016 and 2020 can be understood in this light, a struggle between democracy and its underside, as Tocqueville understood these. The creative democratic culture of America, the fruit of the creative tension that exists between cultural refinement and democratic inclusion, is confronted by the reaction against this creativity.

Tocqueville, Democracy, and Its Underside: Reflections on the Election of Donald Trump

Kamala Harris and Donald Trump in the 2024 election embodied this confrontation. Harris is the child of immigrants. She is an Asian American and a Black American. She is a she, who is a well-educated lawyer with long legal and political experience: as a prosecutor, state attorney general, senator, and vice president. The inclusion that Tocqueville feared, contrary to his expectations, is the material grounds for her democratic promise.

Donald Trump is Harris's opposite. The way he resists democratic inclusion informs his authoritarian politics. He and his family have a record of xenophobia and racism. His father, Fred Trump, was arrested after a Ku Klux Klan rally in Queens, New York in 1927, and just before World War II, he supported the original America First movement and apparently flirted with the antisemitic, Nazi-affiliated German Bund.[41] Father and son were sued by the United States Justice Department in 1973 for racial discrimination against Black people. Trump inherited his wealth and became a power broker in Manhattan real estate. He used his reputation for this work to become a national celebrity as a reality TV billionaire, and then he deftly used the visibility and skills he developed in that role to become president of the United States. In subtle and not so subtle ways, he played on the fears of significant segments of the American electorate: fears of powerful women, the educated, foreigners, African Americans, Asians, Latinos, and much more. He also promised easy solutions to complex problems, such as the challenges of globalization and the suffering it causes, foreign and domestic, the wars in the Middle East, and between Ukraine and Russia, while ignoring other challenges, from viral infections to climate change.

Trump is a man of the dark side of democratic culture, mass culture, that Tocqueville foresaw and lamented: a despot "that democracy has to fear the most," as he put it. Harris is a woman that Tocqueville didn't foresee, a democratic leader who draws on the strengths of democratic inclusiveness. Through the lens of Tocqueville, the political contest between them became a contest between the perils and promise of democratic culture.

First the facts, post 2024 election. Trump and congressional Republicans won a decisive victory, but it was not a landslide. Less than two percent of the vote separated Trump and Harris. In comparison to the 2020 contest, Trump's share of the vote increased just about everywhere. While he increased or at least maintained his margin of victory in his strongholds, he also increased his margin of victory in Democratic districts, regions, and states. The Republicans narrowly won the House of Representative (220 to 215) and won the Senate (53 to 47).

These facts, their causes and the consequences has opened meaningful debates, more immediate and heated among Democrats and their supporters to their left and their right, more subtle, but no less significant among Republicans and their supporters, particularly over the policies that the election results mandate.

Among Democrats: a debate has raged. Why did Harris lose? Why did Trump win? What is to be done to control the most negative consequences of the Trump victory? And what is to be done to not only defeat Trump and his Republican supporters in upcoming elections, but also what must be done to decisively vanquish the threat of Trumpism to American democracy?

Accounts of why Harris lost include misogyny and racism, failing to fully embrace the progressive agenda, or too fully embracing this agenda, for insufficiently taking credit for

Biden's economic, social, and environmental achievements, or for not distinguishing herself from his policies, strikingly in continuing to support the armament of Israel in its war in Gaza. She lost because somehow working-class Americans did not understand how Trump's policies have and will hurt them economically, and how Biden's helped, i.e., it was a problem of communication.

Among Republicans: the decisive victory provides an opportunity to turn the election into a transformative one. There is an appreciation that their Party is becoming the Party of the working class, the less educated, without college degrees, those most challenged by globalization, least prepared to operate in the new economy. But it is still the Party of the most wealthy, the new oligarchs, for pro-business tax cuts, deregulation, and anti-union policies, favored by Wall Street and corporations.

There is a tension between traditional Republican positions, old time Republicanism, i.e., the moral majority, small government, low taxes, favoring strong international commitments, and free trade, and new Republican policies, pro-active support of the victims of globalization, nationalist isolationism, cutting taxes but also radically increasing them in the form of tariffs, focused against political friends and foes alike.

There is an appreciation that alternative media (from Fox News to bro podcasts) are the strength of Trump and the Trumpists, while the legacy media, (from CBS, NBC, and ABC to *The New York Times*, *The Washington Post*, but also *The Wall Street Journal*, with its traditional conservative editorial page) are "the enemy of the people." Trump's appointments confirm this new landscape, as do his executive orders, but there is a persistent question of how far this will go. Will factual truth evaporate? Will objective reporting be discarded? Will the truth be defined by the powers, and not by attempts at objective reporting and critical reasoning from a variety of perspectives? I see a major challenge on the political right between conservatism and Trumpism, explored more fully below.

The challenge for Democrats is to intelligently respond to their defeat. To reconnect with the working class, and to sustain its position as the party of inclusive democratic commitment. The challenge for the Republicans is: will the remnants of the old guard resist the escalating excesses of Trumpism, or will they be overwhelmed?

These challenges constitute the present state of democracy in America. The fate of the Republic is at issue. The Republican victory presents a clear and present danger of regime change, which will be explored in the following chapters. The re-election of Donald Trump may not be just a new administration, a new government with different policies on immigration, taxation, and climate change. The relationship between truth and politics may be transformed. A post-truth regime is apparently emerging. Collaboration for and against the emerging regime, in my judgment, will decide the fate of democracy in America. Understanding this requires a careful consideration of collaboration and a closer examination of the American political landscape. And I believe, an appreciation of the beauty of the gray and the importance of a radical center that is open to democratic actors of the left, right, and center, for both practical and principled reasons, is of crucial importance.

8. A Collaborator: To Be or Not to Be?

This chapter is based upon a Democracy Seminar *symposium I organized on December 3, 2021, as well as the last lecture I gave at the American University of Afghanistan on December 12, 2024. In both settings, I sought to address the ironies of collaboration. Democracies can't survive with it; they also can't survive without it. I open here with a case study of collaboration in a now collapsed regime, the Polish People's Republic, which before the collapse seemed permanent. I close with my reflections and concerns about the fate of the oldest of modern liberal democracies, which I fear may be passing, the United States of America. I analyze collaboration in these two contexts guided by two classic essays: Adam Michnik's "The New Evolutionism" and Václav Havel's "The Power of the Powerless." Michnik and Havel were two of my key guides in understanding the culture of politics and the politics of culture around the old Communist bloc. Here I apply their lessons as I work to make sense of politics and culture much closer to home.*

Collaborating with the enemy is a political *offense*. After Nazism, after Communism, after colonialism, those who have worked with the hated regime have been vilified, often for good reasons, sometimes too hastily. Yet also, in the face of a common enemy, collaboration is a *necessity*. Political factions have needed to bury their differences and collaborate, to create a united front against the Nazis, the Communists, the colonialists, the Trumpists. This is an instance in which an inevitable dilemma of the social condition is fused into language. It's an ongoing puzzle: with whom should one collaborate? when to collaborate? how to collaborate?

A Case Study of Collaboration

I observed this dilemma as a student of post-war Poland. During Communist rule, these questions dynamically appeared once open-armed resistance to the new order receded. When is it wise and appropriate to collaborate with the regime, hoping to make it somewhat more humane, somewhat more responsive to the interests, concerns, and commitments of the Polish people, and when is such collaboration out of the question because it would further empower the regime and lend to it unearned legitimacy? When is collaboration sincere and principled, a basis for some hope? And when is it a cynical act in pursuit of self-interest? And further, what are the anticipated and unanticipated consequences of collaboration? These were the pressing questions in post-war Poland, but they are not only Polish questions I remind myself as Donald Trump is again president of the United States of America.

During the Stalinist period in Poland, from 1948 until 1956, there was one Catholic organization that collaborated with the Communist regime, PAX, the so-called progressive Catholic organization, headed by Bronisław Piasecki, ironically (or perhaps not), the leader of the Young Fascist League in the 1930s. He actively collaborated with the Stalinist regime while the head of the Catholic Church in Poland, Cardinal Stefan Wyszyński, was in prison and while a systematic attack on church properties and privileges were ongoing. Piasecki was a collaborator in the negative sense, as was Quisling in Norway, he so clearly so that his name identifies this type of collaboration.

But it is not always so clear. In 1956 in Poland, after the death of Stalin and after workers' strikes in the city of Poznań, a more patriotic, post-Stalinist, less repressive regime formed. The workers and the ruling party didn't push as hard for radical change as their counterparts in Hungary, where revolt led to Soviet tanks and violent repression. The ascendant reformist leader of the Party, Władysław Gomułka, negotiated a moderate liberalization with the society and with the Soviets, a "Polish road to socialism," conciliating with the Catholic Church, turning away from collectivization of agriculture, and enacting more liberal cultural policies. This forestalled a Soviet invasion, and it presented new possibilities for previously excluded groups to become politically active. As Cardinal Wyszyński was released from prison and established a modus vivendi with the regime, two lay Catholic groups engaged: *Więź* and *Znak*. They collaborated with rulers with whom they had the most fundamental of disagreements because they judged that the regime was not disappearing for the foreseeable future. They defended Catholic principles and interests, adding their viewpoints in constituting the order of things, making Communist rule somewhat more pluralistic. Theirs was very much a gray approach.

In 1968, such calculations were unsettled. The relatively moderate (in comparison with its fraternal ruling parties around the old bloc) policies of the Polish Party, seeking to balance liberalization with orthodoxy and fealty to the Soviets, reached an impasse. Gomułka's leadership was under attack from the left and the right. "Revisionists" called for more liberal economic policies and for "Marxist humanist" ideological reforms, while a more nationalist wing of the Party, associated with veterans' organizations, pushed against cultural liberalism and "cosmopolitanism." These intra-party struggles came out in the open when a play, a dramatization of the nineteenth-century national classic, *Forefathers Eve*, at the National Theater in Warsaw, was shut down, rumor had it at the insistence of the Soviet embassy. Students protested, first in Warsaw led by Adam Michnik among others, and then around the country. They were then brutally repressed.

An antisemitic purge followed, thinly veiled as anti-Zionist, for example, "Kowalik's" given name was revealed as being "Grynburg," and he was subsequently fired. Tens of thousands of Polish Jews, most of the remaining survivors after the Holocaust, fled or were pushed out of the country, along with other prominent liberal intellectuals, who were not Jewish, such as Leszek Kołakowski.

Collaboration became more challenging. With the crackdown and the purge, collaboration no longer offered principled rewards for the regime's most radical critics. It became clear, for example, to Michnik and Jacek Kuroń (the man that Michnik recognized as his teacher and the co-author of an important Marxist critique of Communist practice using official ideology), that using Marxism, the official ideology, to criticize official practice no longer made sense. They no longer thought, spoke about, and dedicated their lives to a Marxist approach to democracy, humanism, and justice, rather they thought, spoke, and dedicated themselves to each ideal apart from the official ideology. They judged that collaboration with the regime had become more problematic, while collaboration with those who shared antipathy towards the regime, those who they previously viewed as opponents, as their intellectual and political "other," became appealing. This is the context of Michnik's *Kościół, lewica, dialog* ("The Church, the left, dialogue," analyzed in chapter 3), as well as his seminal essay, "The New Evolutionism."

In that essay, Michnik expresses appreciation for the past accomplishments of *Znak* and *Więź* (he names them neo-positivists, referring to a nineteenth-century Polish approach to nationalism), and for revisionist critics, such as himself, who used official ideology to push for a more humanistic socialism. Yet, reflecting on the changing post-1968 landscape, he points to a gray, radically centrist, strategy: not reform led by the Party, as was the strategy in Czechoslovakia in 1968, not revolution from below, as was the strategy in Hungary in 1956, but evolution from below in which the society, workers, and intellectuals, address each other, not primarily to change Party leadership and policy, rather, seeking change among themselves to which the Party must respond. Here, he saw a different role for the Church, beyond frontal resistance to or collaboration with the regime:

> The Church hierarchy's consistently and specifically anti-Communist position, in which all social and political changes that have taken place since 1945 were rejected, has been evolving into a more broadly anti-totalitarian stance. Jeremiads against "godless ones" have given way to documents quoting the principles of the Declaration of Human Rights; in pastoral letters, Polish bishops have been defending the right to truth and standing up for human freedom and dignity. Most important, they have been defending the civil liberties of the working people, and particularly their right to strike and to form independent labor unions. The Catholic Church, which consistently resists pressure from the government.

> The Catholic Church, which consistently resists pressure from the government and defends Christian principles as well as the principles of the Declaration of Human Rights, has necessarily become a place where attitudes of nonconformity and dignity among the people can mingle. It is therefore a key source of encouragement for those who seek to broaden civil liberties.[42]

This is a remarkable essay, anticipating with clear understanding the changes that were emerging in Poland and around the Soviet bloc in 1980s. An extensive alternative public life was constituted in Poland, with a substantial democratic opposition, crystalizing in the mass independent labor movement,

Solidarność, which ultimately contributed to the collapse of the Soviet Empire. There were similar though less extensive developments among Poland's neighbors.

The context of the essay: A workers' strike in 1970 centered in the city of Gdansk, intellectual protests against constitutional reforms that officially recognized the subservience of the Polish public to the Party and the Polish Party to the Soviets in 1976, followed by another wave of workers' protests centered in the city of Radom, the establishment of the Committee to Defend Workers, which led to a new form of class collaboration, free of vanguardism of the Communist tradition and the elitism of patriotic imagination. I have already given an overview of these developments in chapter 3, now a key observation: the emerging alternative public in Poland presented intriguing dilemmas not only for those who were most politically active, the church and leftist critics of the regime. They also were part of the daily life of less politically engaged people, including people who attempted to stay clear of politics.

The cultural life of Communist Poland was under the control of the Party. If poets wanted to reach an audience beyond their immediate social circles, they had to face the review of the censor. There was no theater without official review, as there was no science and scholarship free of official control. To be sure, it was possible to game the censor, for artists and scholars to write between the lines and for readers to read those lines, and for the censors to choose to ignore what most often they certainly understood was their meaning. Agreeing to play this game was a form of passive collaboration with the political order.

With the development of alternative public space, a collaborative choice presented itself: to continue playing the official game, or to operate apart from it. Initially, the independent public space was quite marginal, starting with a *Bulletin of Information* reporting on the repression of striking workers and marshalling social support for them and their families, but from this small start, many journals, magazines, books, publishing houses, independent and educational initiatives developed.

From the point of view of those most committed to independent developments, work inside official institutions then appeared as a form of collaboration in the negative sense, a passive negative collaboration. In contrast, they collaborated with each other, working to expand social and cultural life apart from officialdom. This required collaboration among people with different and often conflicting interests, between town and country, across class lines, between the secular and the religious, the left and the right. This was the broad social implication of Michnik's "new evolutionism," the actual historical developments that the essay anticipated.

From the point of view of those who continued to work within official institutions, most out of perceived necessity, the work in alternative spaces appeared to be marginal, an active positive collaboration that they judged was bound to be inconsequential. The public was small and confined to elites and privileged groups in major cities. *Solidarność* challenged this calculation. The two sides of collaboration, then, were operating, and choosing between them was not clear and simple. When the workers of Poland created *Solidarność*, the positive prospects of collaborating within a pluralistic society became an imperative, even in the face of repression, which came with the declaration of martial law.

Thus, the decision whether to collaborate with the regime or to refuse to collaborate had significant twists and turns in Poland. There and then, collaboration constituted and responded to its specific historical development. Choosing to actively collaborate with the opposition was a significant step, for some a necessity, for others, even if they had sympathy for those taking the step, it was too difficult.

Collaboration and "The Power of the Powerless" in Everyday Life

Michnik's Czech friend and colleague, Václav Havel, a new evolutionist comrade in arms, examined collaboration more closely, specifically the seamy side of passive collaboration, analyzing how the dilemmas of collaboration appear in the everyday life of the broad public and analyzing their consequences. As was true with Michnik's work, the specific context of the case is Communist Europe, but it has broad application.

Havel had a remarkable career. He was a leading Czech dramatist in the 1960s, who received international attention. I first came across his work when I was studying alternative theater in New York City, before I had any special interest in East Central Europe. In the 1970s, Havel became a leader in the Czech opposition, one of the founding members of Charter 77. It was then that he wrote his most famous essay, "The Power of the Powerless." In 1989, he led the movement that overthrew the Communist regime, then becoming the first president of post-Communist Czechoslovakia and with the split of the country, the first president of the Czech Republic. But when he wrote his essay, far from such political heights, he focused on the everyday experiences of a common man, facing a fundamental and nearly universal question: to be or not to be a collaborator.

The essay centers around a dramatic scene. Havel tells the story of a greengrocer who is obligated to put up a sign with the slogan "Workers of the World Unite" along with the fruits and vegetables in his shop window. Each morning, when the grocer displays his wares in the window, he must put up the sign. Putting up the sign is a thoughtless act. The grocer may or may not have read *The Communist Manifesto*, from which the slogan became an integral part of the worker class movement, a key rallying cry first of the socialist movement, then of Communist states. Havel imagines, quite realistically, that none of this is on the mind of the grocer, as he goes about his daily business. Putting the sign in the window involves as much thought as putting an apple or an onion in the window. The grocer does, though, fully understand what would happen if he doesn't put the sign up. Havel notes:

> I think it can safely be assumed that the overwhelming majority of shopkeepers never think about the slogans they put in their windows, nor do they use them to express their real opinions. That poster was delivered to our greengrocer from the enterprise headquarters along with the onions and carrots. He put them all into the window simply because it has been done that way for years, because everyone does it, and because that is the way it has to be. If he were to refuse, there could be trouble. He could be reproached for not having the proper decoration in his window; someone might even accuse him of disloyalty. He does it because these things must be done if one is to get along in life. It is one of the thousands of details that guarantee him a relatively tranquil life "in harmony with society," as they say.[43]

Havel goes on to show that the greengrocer sign is one passive collaborative act, a little piece of a whole that confers legitimacy to the ideological system. Ordinary subjects of the system vote in meaningless elections, in which Party candidates receive 99% of the vote. They sign petitions in favor of Party positions. They don't speak their minds in public gatherings, mouthing the slogans of officialdom instead. And each subject does this as they observe others doing the same. In this way, a system of legitimation through disbelief is established, as I analyzed systematically in *Beyond Glasnost: The Post-Totalitarian Mind.*

When the shopkeeper puts the sign up, he is safe. The people around him see in his act not a commitment to a grand political project. They hardly notice the sign and don't consider the pros and cons of its declaration. Rather they see life as usual, compliance with the order of things: a small act of collaboration.

Havel illuminates the two sides of the everyday collaboration coin. By first describing how it works:

> The greengrocer had to put the slogan in his window, therefore, not in the hope that someone might read it or be persuaded by it, but to contribute, along with thousands of other slogans, to the panorama that everyone is very much aware of. This panorama, of course, has a subliminal meaning as well: it reminds people where they are living and what is expected of them. It tells them what everyone else is doing and indicates to them what they must do as well, if they don't want to be excluded, to fall into isolation, alienate themselves from society, break the rules of the game, and risk the loss of their peace and tranquility and security.[44]

And then he enumerates what happens when collaboration in the negative sense is replaced by collaboration in the positive sense, when collaboration with the regime is replaced by collaboration with those who dare to work against the regime. Punishment is soon forthcoming, but so is the power of the powerless:

> Let us now imagine that one day something in our greengrocer snaps and he stops putting up the slogans merely to ingratiate himself. He stops voting in elections he knows are a farce.

He begins to say what he really thinks at political meetings. And he even finds the strength in himself to express solidarity with those whom his conscience commands him to support. In this revolt the greengrocer steps out of living within the lie. He rejects the ritual and breaks the rules of the game. He discovers once more his suppressed identity and dignity. He gives his freedom a concrete significance. His revolt is an attempt to live within the truth.

The bill is not long in coming. He will be relieved of his post as manager of the shop and transferred to the warehouse. His pay will be reduced. His hopes for a holiday in Bulgaria will evaporate. His children's access to higher education will be threatened. His superiors will harass him and his fellow workers will wonder about him. Most of those who apply these sanctions, however, will not do so from any authentic inner conviction but simply under pressure from conditions, the same conditions that once pressured the greengrocer to display the official slogans.[45]

In this way, the two sides of collaboration were present in the everyday life of society. When the greengrocer and anyone else puts the sign up in the window, votes for the Communist candidate, uses the official language in a community meeting or in their application for admission into a school, a workplace, or a passport, they collaborate in the negative sense of the term. Havel further underscores that not only such applicants, but also those who judge them, those who are in power, from the lowest level apparatchiks to the head of the Communist Party, are involved in the same game. They will justify any decision using the official logic and language. The logical conclusion from this is that everyone contributes to the panorama, from the highest Party official to those who just want to get through the challenges of ordinary life, all live in the lie, perpetuate the lie that is the Communist system.

When they don't and specifically when they don't along with others, they collaborate in an entirely different way. This is the hidden power of the apparently powerless. The power that was behind *Solidarność*, to cite the prime example.

The two forms of collaboration raise a whole series of ethical and political challenges. Do all the greengrocers of the world have an ethical responsibility to refuse putting the sign "workers of the world unite" in their shop windows? If they don't, are they no better than "quislings" such as Piasecki of PAX in Stalinist Poland? Beyond Havel's story, this question has devastating implications. He starkly suggests that to put the sign up means that you are living a lie, to not put it up, means that then, and only then, you are living in the truth.

Overt, cynical collaborators, such as Piasecki, "the progressive Catholic," in post-war Poland, are a threat to a principled political order, but so are passive collaborators, such as the compliant grocer and those who game the system to provide for themselves, and their colleagues, friends, and loved ones a peaceful private life, as Havel demonstrates.

Yet, I believe that we can and should go beyond Havel's story. First, there is the general issue. Havel suggests that there is an imperative for ordinary people to absolutely avoid collaboration with a system they do not support. He highlights how, every day, relatively passive collaboration, has huge unintended consequences, both sustaining a problematic system and compromising individual integrity. He doesn't consider the serious private consequences of refusing to passively collaborate. It is not at all clear that it is always wrong to first protect those who are closest to you, your close colleagues, friends, and family, to serve a public good. Commitment to an abstract public good over the commitment to those who are near and dear to you would be very problematic: commitment to humanity but not to specific people.

Further, even if we recognize this built-in tension in political life, a primary instance of the social condition we have been considering here, there is an additional problem: public life is rarely so clear, so black and white, as he imagines in his classic text. Sometimes small gestures of loyalty to officialdom opens space for exploring alternatives to the dominant order, or even opposing the social order, and such a gray zone is a normal aspect of social life in the previously existing socialist order in which Havel and Michnik worked, but also far beyond that world.

Both Michnik's positivists and revisionists worked in this zone: the former, by accepting the legitimacy of the official social institutions while attempting to use these institutions to pursue political goals different from those of the Communist Party, the latter by using the official ideology (Marxism) to criticize official institutions. Both, in a sense, put the sign "workers of the world unite" in their shop windows to attempt to do things that the people who gave them the sign did not anticipate or desire. And Michnik underscores that these unanticipated consequences were the grounds for broad political developments beyond Party control and direction.

We have considered two different kinds of collaboration in the context of a regime that is perceived to be illegitimate: collaboration with the regime, and collaboration against the regime. We have observed that these forms of collaboration are not only a matter of the activities of political elites but also of people in their everyday lives. I think it is important, nonetheless, to recognize the difference between active cynical collaborators such as Piasecki and the passive greengrocers of the world. There is a striking contrast in the intentionality and therefore responsibility. I note here the parallel between Havel's examination of the responsibilities of the greengrocer and Hannah Arendt's notion of the banality of evil.

Totalitarian orders result from complex interactions between true belief and cynicism, as we will examine in the next chapter. They are buttressed by combinations of active cynical collaborators and more passive ones, fully aware cynics and more thoughtless ones, political leaders and apparently powerless people, who have more power than they think. I am deeply concerned that these combinations are moving my country in profoundly anti-democratic directions.

Collaboration in Trump's America

The kind of collaborative opposition to Trump that immediately emerged in the opening of his first term in office did not develop with his re-election. Instead of passionately opposing Trump and the Trumpists, many former activists initially retreated from political engagement. Given that Trump did unambiguously win the election, the protest was slow in coming. As he took office, the opposition to Trump 2.0 was more muted and diffuse than the first time around.

As mass deportations became a reality, as Trump and Elon Musk have eviscerated the federal work force, attempting to dismantle the administrative state, not only pardoning all those who were involved in the attack on the United States Capitol on January 6, 2020, but investigating all those who took part in the prosecution of the attackers, official opposition from local, state, and national authorities was not nearly as unified as it was in the past.

In the opening days of Trump's Presidency, USAID, the United States Agency for International Development became public enemy # 1. Elon Musk, effectively the co-president in the first months of the Trump regime, called the primary agency for distributing humanitarian and pro-democracy aid a criminal organization and proposed "feeding USAID into a woodchipper" This created a global humanitarian disaster, as it threatened the standing of the United States around the world. The United States surrendered in the battle of soft power with its adversaries. And as the foreign strongmen from around the world celebrated the move, there has been little pushback by Republicans. They have collaborated enthusiastically or cynically, with cynicism turning into enthusiasm and the other way around (more on the workings of cynicism in the age of Trump in chapter 9).

Environmental and consumer protections have been attacked. The independence of the news media, law firms, and universities have been challenged, and a series of apparently coordinated unconstitutional expansions of executive power have created a constitutional crisis, in the judgment of leading legal scholars. It took some time for social protests to this threat to develop, and when a forceful response to mass deportations developed, Trump called in the troops.

The Democratic Party's opposition to Trump was hesitant, to the dismay of many of its supporters. Congressional leaders even accepted the appointment of incompetents and deeply flawed human beings to run his administration. Among them were television celebrities and close relatives with no relevant expertise, his defense attorneys, and accused sexual predators. There was an acceptance of the inevitable, with a wait and see attitude being the prevailing initial response.

Most concerning, Trumpism has become acceptable to a larger portion of the population. It's been normalized. Donald Trump's indecency and vulgarity have been celebrated by many, overlooked by many more. When he has used extreme rhetoric, some reveled in his extremism, while many other supporters haven't taken him seriously. Trump's bizarre proposals to take back the Panama Canal by force or buy Greenland have been mostly met by incredulity and silence. As it is often noted, "people took him seriously but not literally," when he called for the prosecution of his perceived enemies, including distinguished political leaders, along with doctors, scientists, journalists, and academics, and when he promised one really violent day to solve the problem of property crime. Trump is being Trump when he threatens to leave NATO, when he invited Putin to punish NATO Allies "who don't pay their bills," when he called global warming a scam, and when he deliberately attacked and undermined the independence of the free press and universities. His threats and exaggerations were discounted by many, if not most, who support him, while somehow they did continue to believe his promises of economic prosperity and border security, without concerning themselves with the details and implications of tariffs and mass deportations. (The belief in his economic promises may be his key Achilles heel.)

In sum, oppositional collaboration did not match Trump's forceful repressive actions, and acceptance of the regime's normality has been more widespread. These developments have been coupled with a frightening emergence of collaboration with the anti-democratic threat, among politicians of both political parties, leaders of the news media, and among foreign leaders. I see a remarkable similarity between the ways leaders and publics have responded to Trumpism, and the ways collaborators responded to twentieth-century modern tyrannies, such as the ones Havel, Michnik, and Arendt have examined.

Democratic Collaborators: they have faced a series of collaborative dilemmas. For the most part, they have stood in opposition to Donald Trump's policies, and have opposed his most problematic nominees. Yet, they have been caught between their campaign assertions that a Trump presidency presents a unique challenge to democracy in America, and their commitment to the peaceful transfer of power, recognizing that Donald Trump legitimately won the election.

Thus, a prime early example, the very awkward meeting between Biden and Trump on November 13, 2024, soon after the election day, in which Biden upheld the performative traditions and offered "everything we can to make sure you're accommodated, have what you need." He offered complete cooperative collaboration. Such collaboration was in stark contrast with Biden's earlier assertions that Donald Trump presented an existential threat to the future of America's democratic traditions and practices.

If his earlier assertions, which became central to his and Kamala Harris's presidential campaign, were sincere, and I believe they were, then it would appear that Biden's post-election performance involved collaboration, in the negative sense, with a man and a movement that he and most Democrats believe will profoundly challenge, perhaps destroy, American democracy. The tension between these two Biden stances compactly represent the problems Democrats more broadly have faced since Trump's victory.

And there is the political paradox, whether the Democrats collaborate with each other against Trump and Trumpism, or they follow tradition and collaborate with President Trump, their collaboration potentially weakens democracy, despite their intentions. It's a weakening of democracy beyond their control. By collaborating with each other, working against Trump, they confirm the Manichean view of Trumpists that the elites, the media, and the deep state are moving against the popular will of the majority that elected Trump and his Republican supporters. They would further the polarization of the United States and likely would motivate those who have their hands on the rungs of power to use them. Yet, by recognizing the popular will that supported Trump, and then collaborate with him, even to a limited degree, they give some legitimacy to the worst of Trump's excesses. Navigating this paradox has both political and ethical dimensions (echoing the ethical dilemmas Max Weber illuminated in his "Politics as a Vocation"). Politically, it is a matter of judging which form of collaboration is more likely to reduce the threats Trump presents. The ethics of collaboration center around one being true to one's patriotic commitment in upholding the conventions and traditions of democracy by giving some support to the legitimately elected powers, conceived as a new administration, or working to weaken the elected powers, conceived as a new anti-democratic regime (which I think it is, as explained in chapter 7 and explored more fully in the concluding chapters).

The dilemma has first appeared for Democrats in the advice and consent process of Trump's governmental nominations. It has persisted as Democrats have weighed the balance between loyalty and opposition in their role as "the loyal opposition." Should Democratic governors, mayors, and other state and local officials collaborate with Trump on the issue of immigration, or should they attempt to "Trump proof" their states and localities? How forcefully should they try to reject his most egregious policies and grab for power. The latter, ironically, requires collaboration with Republicans. The Democrats' calculation of their own political interests, and the safety and well-being of their constituency and the broader public determines their decision-making.

There is an ethical dimension for the Democrats, but not nearly as severe as the ethical challenge Republicans face. The Democrats are operating in a gray zone, weighing the best way to oppose Trumpism, leaning more on opposition, or leaning more on loyalty to the conventions of democratic practice. There is no ideal way to proceed. They don't face stark choices such as the one Havel's greengrocer faced. The Republicans do.

Republican Collaborators: their ethical challenges have been deeper and have been more consequential. The problems first appeared with Trump's campaign and subsequent victory in 2016. The response to Trump was initially straight-forward. In that he was outside the Republican Party consensus, many, if not most, Republican political leaders, including his primary opponents, openly and forcefully criticized him. They stood against the positions he took on free trade and immigration, his open authoritarianism, and his racist and misogynist attacks on Barack Obama and Hillary Clinton. They stood against his vulgarity and his refusal to commit to supporting the Republican nominee if he didn't prevail. Vice President J. D. Vance publicly called him an idiot and reprehensible, and privately compared him to Hitler. Secretary of State Marco Rubio denounced him as a con artist and described his style of leadership as dangerous. Ted Cruz, in 2024, one of Trump's most enthusiastic supporters in the Senate, who was dedicated to the quick approval of all his nominees, refused to support him at the 2016 Republican nominating convention after a bitter primary campaign.

While, in 2016, Trump ran against the Republican Party establishment, by 2024 he embodied it. His opponents in 2016 failed to collaborate among themselves against Trump to forestall his victory. Subsequently, they have competed to collaborate with him. They have worked carefully to stay in his favor. They have sought ritualistically an audience with him to garner his support. And when it comes to policy, for almost all of them, his wish has been their command.

Reports from journalists indicate that among Republican leaders, there have been many who privately have confided off the record that they have great reservations about Trump's policies and personality, but they, nonetheless, publicly have supported him in order to survive politically or to achieve one substantive goal or another, be that banning abortion or deregulating the petroleum industry. They have further rationalized that if they were not inside the Trump tent, others without their critical convictions would hold authority and be much worse. They have put the MAGA sign in their window and have contributed to the redefinition of their Party, to a transformation of the American political landscape, and to a redefinition of themselves. The Party has become an anti-democratic, post-truth Party, led by post-truth leaders, supported by post-truth constituents. This starts with cynical collaboration, leading to collaborative conviction, empowering cynical manipulation, all centered around an odd cult of personality.

The personality of Donald Trump now centers the Republican Party, and apart from a few slogans and authoritarian instincts, his political commitments are thin and elastic. Suspicious of foreigners, he seeks to close the border. Suspicious of other countries and customs, he views international relations as a zero-sum game, where "they" are taking advantage of "us." Caught in a hazy nostalgia for a lost ideal moment in history, (I think the imaginative one is stuck in the popular culture of the 1950s, the era of "Father Knows Best"), his guiding principles are commitments to "America First" and to "Make America Great Again," which mean whatever he has asserted them to mean. The leader has made wild policy shifts, and his followers follow accordingly. I am struck how this loyalty, the agreement to collaborate with him under any and all circumstances, rivals the loyalty of Communist Party members to Stalin's Party of the 1930s and 1940s.

I am not asserting that Trump is a new Stalin, or that Trumpism is somehow a new version of Stalinism. Trump is a distinctively twenty-first-century tyrant (more on this in the concluding chapters). Crucially, there are formal similarities between tyrants past and present, when it comes to the assertion of truth, and those who collaborate to confirm the assertion, most evident in the events of January 6, 2021, and the rationalizations that followed.

Soon after the events, Trump's supporters asserted that the attack on the Capitol Building, with the wild chants of "Hang Mike Pence," breaking windows, breaking down doors, invading offices and defacing the building, attacking Capitol police, resulting in critical injuries and death, was the work of leftist provocateurs, "antifa." Then Trump's supporters asserted that the event was little more than a class trip, a peaceful march, a picnic. They minimized the atrocities that our lying eyes perceived on live TV, including harrowing imagines of the vice president and members of Congress, including strong Trump supporters, fleeing for safety from mob violence. The president watched the explosion of violence and disruption silently, without intervening to stop his supporters for hours. He then praised their commitment to a righteous cause but quieted them down. Then he minimized the violence, and then he celebrated the righteous cause, promised to free political prisoners who were locked up for their actions that fateful day, and delivered on his promise. Given that he never recognized the fact that he lost the 2020 election, he had to take this action. Notably, this is now the official truth. Republicans conform and collaborate, some cynically, others sincerely. I will analyze the move from the cynical to the sincere and back in chapter 9. But before I do, we should consider collaboration of the broader public.

Beyond Democrats and Republicans, all around the United States and the world, people are putting the equivalent of the greengrocer's sign in their windows, while others are refusing to do so.

Official Collaborators: Governors, and other state and local officials, on the one hand, are preparing to work with federally mandated deportations, in red states with conviction. On the other hand, officials in blue states collaborate to avoid damage from the Trumpist wave and attempt to turn back the wave. Collaboration is both positive and negative.

Corporate Collaborators: Most disturbing is the collaboration from "the liberal media." Even before the Trump triumph, the owners of two major newspapers, *The Washington Post* and *The Los Angeles Times*, killed their editors' endorsements of Kamala Harris, foreseeing Trump's victory, with the *Los Angeles Times* going further after the fact, limiting negative opinion pieces about Trump and Trumpism. Disney Corporation, the corporate owner of one of the three major broadcast networks in the United States, settled a frivolous defamation lawsuit against ABC News, which in the judgment of experts they most likely would have won. Trump even sued a pollster who mistakenly forecasted a Harris victory in the state of Iowa. Trump's deeds are matching his words, as he depicted the media "the enemy of the people," and much of the media is bending to his will. I know from my experience behind the Iron Curtain that self-censorship often works more effectively than official censorship, a pattern we can now observe in the United States.

And "tech barons," along with other leaders of major American corporations, have anxiously sought meetings with Trump after his election, and before his inauguration generously contributing to the costs of the ceremonies. People who in the past made clear their opposition to Trump and Trumpism have gone on to put the MAGA sign in neon lights in their shop windows, seeking to profit in the process.

Abroad: The two faces of collaboration have been observable among the political leadership of the United States' (former?) allies. Leaders have recognized that Trump is changing the rules of the international order, and they know they must accommodate the new direction of the United States or to collaborate with each other to work against it. They are facing dilemmas resembling Trump's opponents in the United States. The leaders of Canada and Mexico, proceeding somewhat differently, have sought to minimize the threat of draconian tariffs, pursuing their national interests, and confirming their national identity. The president of Ukraine, Volodymyr Zelenskyy, realizing that it is far from certain that the United States will continue to support the defense of his country, has tried to change its stated war aims in such a way that they articulate with MAGA ideology. The nation members of NATO and the European Union, likewise, have worked to sustain United States support in ways that appear to mirror Trump's agenda, specifically by increasing their national contributions to NATO. Given American wealth and power European leaders will define their relations with the United States using MAGA slogans or at a minimum not clearly questioning the slogans.

The MAGA signs will be put in foreign ministry windows around the world; until they aren't. At some point, the cynical compliance with the new regime will reach its limits, or the calculation of interest and national identity will require clear noncompliance. And as with the greengrocer, the consequences are potentially immense. Collaboration with or against Trump has both national and international consequences.

Collaboration and the Dark Side of a New "New Evolutionism"

Michnik, in "The New Evolutionism" understood, in a way that Havel didn't in "The Power of the Powerless," that sometimes collaboration with a despised regime is necessary, a gray insight. Michnik also understood, along with Havel, that at other times it is imperative to cut off collaboration and work to distance oneself from the regime and focus on the constitution of an independent public, to "live in truth" within independent social circles. Deciding when to follow these two paths of collaboration, with and against authority, is a ubiquitous challenge. Making that decision wisely, I believe, is predicated upon a political appreciation of the beauty of the gray and of the importance of a fundamental commitment to a center, which is not necessarily a moderate commitment.

I fully appreciated the collaborators with the Communist regime who managed to create zones of independent value despite the control and censorship of the Communists. And I reluctantly appreciate people who collaborate with Donald Trump who seek to modify his political excesses. I am terrified of an unleashed Trump and of Trumpist true believers. When such collaboration is acceptable and when it is not remains an important question with no simple black and white answer. For this reason, though Biden logically contradicted himself when he moved from his campaign position that Trump represents an existential threat to working with him on the peaceful transfer of power, I recognize the ethical and political reasons to do so. Timing matters and deciding on the timing is an ongoing challenge. This is the wisdom of Michnik's "new evolutionism." He understood that deciding with whom to collaborate and when, and how to collaborate as it applied to the last years of the Communist regime was a matter of situational judgment. Those questions are also ours.

Now we are observing a development in the opposite direction, which presents new challenges. While Michnik's is a progressive evolutionism with an independent public space expanding and ultimately challenging the regime, we observe a development in the opposite direction, a regressive evolutionism, with the challenge of wisely responding to it. Michnik perceived a virtuous progressive cycle, with an understanding that the "best" does get in the way of the "better," and that pursuing the better can lead to fundamental improvement. He saw the possibility of significant progress, the defeat of the Communist regime. In the final chapters of this inquiry, I will present an analysis of the regressive dark side of this cycle and consider how this side of things can be avoided.

Conclusions

The appreciation of the beauty of the gray and the radical commitment to a free public life informed the lectures upon which the chapters of this book have been based. Each lecture was a response to an invitation, each my part of dialogues with students, teachers, and colleagues at specific times and places. In the chapters, I have sought to go beyond those times and places, exploring how a gray sensibility and the commitment to the center confront, from different angles, major problems of our times.

In the chapters, step by step, I worked against common assumptions about the social life that stand in the way of addressing our problems: thinking anew about uncertainty (chapter 2), seeking to understand what intellectuals do to make things better, and not worse (chapter 3), grasping the political priority of a free public domain (chapter 4), appreciating the critical role of art (chapter 5), demonstrating the power of "acting as if" in the pursuit of education, human rights, and the rule of law (chapter 6), turning to the American case, exploring how the previously "leader of the free world" has been at the forefront of the retreat of democracy, and how this retreat and the resistance to it have long been built into the fabric of American society (chapter 7), and in chapter 8, considering how the promise and perils of collaboration set the stage for the ongoing struggle to turn back the retreat.

In the concluding chapters, I open with the simple description of the global retreat, and I then analyze its dimensions and how cynicism is contributing to it (chapter 9). I close with an examination of hope, showing how a gray sensibility and a radical commitment to the center present possible alternatives to the presently prevailing trends, hope that the present state of affairs will not be extended into our future (chapter 10).

I have a sense that the challenges we are now facing are unprecedented. I fight against despair and know that many of my family, friends, colleagues, and students are in the fight with me, including the readers of this book. In the final two chapters, I am imagining giving two virtual lectures to you, in which I share my thoughts on the implications of my inquiries.

9. The Cynical Society (Revisited) and the Retreat of Democracy

Once upon a time, long, long ago, but also not so long ago, democracy prevailed as a political ideal. Alexis de Tocqueville described it as humanity's inevitable future, for better and for worse, as we have seen in chapter 7. Politicians of the left, right, and center shared the ideal, as they competed on the path to its realization. Even dictators of the left and the right claimed the ideal as their own, or they proposed that their task was to prepare the population for it. Recall the idea of "the dictatorship of the proletariat," leading "people's democracies," and the assertions of reactionary dictators that their role is to educate the population so that it will be ready for the responsibilities of democratic citizenship, for example by the military juntas of Argentina and Chile.

The Retreat

These days democracy is more directly challenged. I observed this firsthand in Afghanistan. The Taliban, and other similar Islamists elsewhere, reject the notion of democracy as a modern import, imposed on the Islamic world by infidels, to be rejected in favor of sharia, as interpreted by informed religious judges. Yet many of the Taliban's opponents are also skeptical about democracy. Given how the promise of democracy has rationalized occupation and corruption in their lived experience, many of my Afghan colleagues are hesitant. They reject the Taliban's rule, though how they do so, how openly, significantly varies. But when it comes to developing ideas for alternatives, there is some reticence about democracy. I found it fruitful to explore with them not democracy as a package, not *liberal democracy*, not *social democracy*, but detailed elements of democracy—the rule of the people, free association and speech, cultural freedom, the equal dignity and inclusion of all citizens regardless of race, ethnicity, religious belief, and gender and sexuality.

My course on democracy, "Thinking About Democracy," was informed by the insights and critical reflections of my co-teachers, including a legal scholar who is seriously engaged in investigating Islamic law, a political scientist who is trying to somehow integrate the ideals of liberal democracy and Islamic rule, a practical public official, and a committed liberal democrat who was a sharp critic of official corruption before the Taliban victory, now silenced by the course of events, not only by the present officials, but also by the pettiness and suspicion among their opponents. Democracy is an idea they find attractive, but it hasn't delivered to them, and they wonder if it ever can.

The disenchantment with democracy, of course, is not only evident in their extreme circumstance. Around the world people have become antagonistic to, bored with, or complacent about democracy, and its institutional, legal, and cultural supports. There is a menu of anti-democratic practices that are ascendant worldwide: resistance to the peaceful transfer of power, politicization of the judiciary, undermining the independence of the press and other news media, attacks on immigrants, and racial, ethnic, religious, and sexual minorities, valorizing a segment of the population as the true nationals, i.e., Poles, Hungarians, Indians, Americans, French, Germans, Afghans, etc., most often the more traditional segment from the countryside, coupled with antagonism to city dwellers, intellectuals, universities, and those with a higher education. This is an anti-elitism of a special sort that often is focused against the majority of the population, especially as this anti-elitism is present along with antagonism to women, the demographic majority, when they pursue roles that go beyond traditional practices. This is a truly global development, including in the largest self-proclaimed democracy, India, and the most powerful democracy, the United States of America. The development is becoming ever more powerful in Europe, East and West, North and South, in Latin America, Africa, and Asia.

And what I find to be most concerning is that among those who are not actively supporting such developments, there is not sufficient concern. I observed with dismay when the political pundits agreed that the call of defending democracy had little appeal, wouldn't be decisive in determining the outcome of the elections of 2024 in the United States, and I was deeply disappointed when it turned out that they were right.

I was also dismayed when many critics of the prevailing order, many of my friends on the left, did not respond forthrightly to the clear and present danger of Donald Trump and Trumpism. They were primarily focused on the injustices of capitalism, racism, and sexism, and most tragically, given Trump's aggressive proposals to ethnically cleanse Gaza, on American policies toward Israel-Palestine. Pushing back against the anti-democratic tide was for them not a major concern. They didn't realize that such pushback is crucial for realizing their substantive goals.

Democracy's retreat has many explanations: the bankruptcy of neo-liberalism, the economic and social consequences of globalization, the rising fear of the other, xenophobia and racism, the confusion about and suspicion of cultural and technological change, and various forms of resentment and conspiracy theories, all intensified by the new media order as it has operated in the shadow of the pandemic.

Crucially, there is also the perennial problem—the distance between democratic promise and purportedly democratic practice, as the experiences of my Afghan colleagues and students dramatically reveal. This distance fuels cynicism, which I believe drives the anti-democratic spiral. No one explanation suffices. But I do think that overcoming cynicism is a pre-condition for turning the tide

Cynicism

> I believe that the single most pressing challenge facing American democracy today is widespread public cynicism.

With these words, I opened *The Cynical Society*, published in 1991. Cynicism concerns me now even more than it did then. Back then, I saw an erosion of political principles: politicians manipulated principles and asserted alternative policy programs to pursue their electoral prospects, and the news media ignored principles and programs, reporting and commenting on politics as if it were only about the competing narrow interests of political leaders. I highlighted the consequence: cynical manipulation and interpretation overshadowed the real political debate that did continue to inform the competition between the two major parties, as well as the minor ones and competing social movements.

Nonetheless, I argued that it was a matter of overshadowing genuine democratic competition, not replacing it. There still was an ongoing debate between liberals and conservatives, more expansive and more minimal views of the role of the state in economic policies, more or less emphasis on individual freedom versus the common good, more or less concern with inequality and the persisting problems of racism and sexism, more or less concern with economic growth and efficiency, all the while there was also an agreement on the legitimacy of the democratic playing field. Thus, I thought that the United States was both a cynical society and a democratic one, which still could and should be contrasted with the much more profoundly cynical societies on the other side of the Iron Curtain.

Cynicism worked more radically on the other side. Over there, both the plurality of interpretive truth and the pursuit of singular factual truth, as we have seen in chapter 4, the relationships between truth and politics that Hannah Arendt emphasized, had evaporated. Cynicism prevailed among the political elite, the ruling party, and their subjects, leading to Communist Party power that was legitimated through disbelief, as I analyzed systematically in *Beyond Glasnost*.

I fear that when it comes to cynicism now, we are all on the other side, with a totalitarian culture and politics a clear and present danger. There is a distinctive combination of collaboration and cynicism yielding a spiraling anti-democratic force, not only presenting an underside of democracy, the judgment I made about the United States in 1991, but a path for democracy's demise. Indeed, I think, that there is a real danger that we are entering a post-democratic age.

The totalitarian culture of the twentieth century was based on true belief, based on a simple account of human history. In the Communist or National Socialist versions, the dynamics of class or race provided the key to understanding the connection between past, present, and future. Understanding the past and the present involved challenges, but the future, in these accounts, was all but certain, "the classless society," "the Thousand-Year Reich," as Arendt analyzed in *The Origins of Totalitarianism*. The Party leader and leadership were called upon to steward the revolutionary forces to achieve the inevitable result. They determined what is the truth. They decided how the official ideology was to be understood and applied. Arendt noted the ironic result. Since the Party could decide what the official truth is, anything it declared as true was true. Truth and conviction evaporated. Cynicism followed. I see a perverse variation on this theme with Trump and his international allies, with a similarly horrible outcome. The starting point is, though, cynicism, not true belief, but their interaction is the same.

Trump starts with cynicism, while he asserts he is speaking the truth with a performed certainty. It is never clear what he actually believes, what he actually will do. He does have core prejudices and fears, and these resonate with his enthusiastic supporters: racism, suspicion of immigrants, specifically from "shithole countries," toxic masculinity, anti-intellectualism, fear that others are ripping him off, and by extension ripping America off, a conviction that there was a time in the unspecified past when America was great. For a long time, I thought this was the immediate post-World War II period, but in the opening months of his presidency, President William McKinley, as he led in the age of United States imperialism and tariffs in the late 1890s, is apparently his ideal. And, crucially more than anything else, Trump does believe in his own power: that he is "the only one who can fix it," even celebrating his absolute power. Referring to himself, he has declared: "long live the king."

Take him seriously, but not literally? Given his attempt to disrupt the American constitutional system of checks and balances, and international agreements and alliances concerning trade, human rights, humanitarian assistance, support of democracy and opposition to autocracies, this may not be wise. One never knows exactly where he stands, but he certainly is acting decisively. And when he decisively acts, it is by definition a success even if the facts disconfirm this, such as in the results of the 2020 election, the economic consequences of his "heroic" attempt to transform the global economic order and his solving the problems of the Middle East.

Yet, beyond his prejudices and obsessions, Trump has cynically changed his politics as it has served his interests. He favored abortion rights, then he strongly opposed them, and then he took a more nuanced position. In 2016, he claimed to be a champion of the LGBTQ+ community; in 2024, he has waged a war against it and against "gender ideology." He negotiated "a perfect trade agreement" with Canada and Mexico during his first term. In 2024, he has waged a tariff war against them, the United States's major trading partners. He has asserted that anything he does is legal, and brazenly does not distinguish between his own financial interests and the national interest. He openly advertises his corruption (for example, the "God Bless America Bible" for only $60) and threatens anyone who questions him.

The project of total power is extraordinary, unprecedented in the history of the United States, but with a strong resemblance to the political world I studied in Communist Europe. He unilaterally has asserted the power to name a body of water, the "Gulf of Mexico" for three hundred years, the "Gulf of America," and when a major news outlet, the Associated Press, didn't comply, he banned it from White House press room and Air Force One. He and his loyal minions declare war on DEI initiatives, public and private. And he blamed such programs as the cause of destructive wildfires in California and a tragic air collision in Washington, DC. Meaning: it's the incompetent Blacks, Latinos, and women who caused these disasters. While Trump has pardoned all who attacked the Capitol Building on January 6, 2021, including convicted violent felons, all who have been involved in the prosecution of his crimes are under suspicion and vulnerable to prosecution;

he has purged those who would question his untrammeled authority, those who do not support his "Make America Great Again"/"America First" agenda. Foreign aid must support the president's will and be free of DEI programs and initiatives, and thus USAID has been eviscerated. Food and medicine have been cut off for those in desperate need. And, close to home for me, after my students have been repressed by the Taliban, their education has been again disrupted by the Trumpists. AUAF was shut down, pending review. The young women and men I have been so proud to teach despite the repressions of a fundamentalist regime lost their access to higher education thanks to Trumpism.

Donald Trump has aggressively amassed great power for himself. I find it remarkable that so many in the general public have enthusiastically supported this, and that others with considerable official power have given it up and supported him. His enthusiastic supporters and facilitators are troubling. But, I believe, it is the odd dynamic relationship between cynicism, truth, and collaboration that explains his rise and suggests the grounds for his possible fall.

Republican officials, and their conventional supporters, have moved from cynicism to true belief. They initially supported Trump as a relatively distasteful means to achieve their substantive ends, with disapproval of the way he conducted himself and his more authoritarian assertions. The religious right realized its goal—the Supreme Court that they voted for, which has overturned the constitutional right to abortion. The wealthy and corporate interests acquired the tax cuts and loosening of government regulations they sought. Like Havel's greengrocer considered in chapter 8, they put up in their shop windows "only Trump can fix it," even when they don't believe it, satisfied that their goals would be reached. But their cynicism opened the door for an unanticipated development.

It has become clear that not only did Trump seriously take himself literally, so did an ever-increasing mass of his core supporters and an emerging MAGA elite. Trump tapped into the authoritarian yearning of those who find the aspects of an open, plural, inclusive society not to their liking. Christian nationalists, anti-intellectuals, xenophobes, homophobes, transphobes, misogynists, and racists, as well as relatively sophisticated authoritarian intellectuals and "tech bros" who now wholeheartedly support the great leader.

Trump is a showman who this diverse crew can and does believe in.

For these people, he is supported not despite his vulgarity and aggression, but because of them. And many have moved from cynical support to true belief, which has yielded an escalating totalitarian ambition, but also a new cynicism of the totalitarian variety. The previously skeptical Marco Rubio has administered the State Department ensuring that each program and every employee adheres to the president's agenda. All programs have been suspended (including AUAF) until the loyalty is confirmed. The African American chair of the Joint Chiefs of Staff, General Charles Q. Brown, was replaced because of his woke focus on diversity, as Secretary of Defense Pete Hegseth put it in his confirmation hearings. Dan Caine, a retired Air Force Lieutenant General, his replacement, achieved his position as an apparent loyalist, who Trump recalls wore a MAGA hat when they first met in Iraq in 2018, contrary to regulations against partisanship in the military. The Attorney General, Kash Patel, has compiled a list of enemies of Trump and the MAGA movement; he is also the author of an absurd children's book series celebrating "King Donald" who prevails, with help of the mighty wizard Kash, against the Russia investigation, the rigging of the 2020 election, and prosecution by the Justice Department.

To paraphrase Marx, the history of art repeats itself, first as tragedy, socialist realism of the twentieth century, now as farce, the MAGA fantasy of the twenty-first, echoing through the bro podcast universe. A culture is emerging which is the very opposite of the art we examined in chapter 5, with Trump himself as a culture czar, chairman of the Board of the Kennedy Center, among his other positions. Rubio, Hegseth, and Patel are committed MAGA apparatchiks, with filial connection with their twentieth-century predecessors.

The claim to total power that Trump has made in the name of Making America Great Again, leads to an intensified cynicism on his part, and on his loyal facilitators. Capricious decisions define the political agenda: retake the Panama Canal, buy Greenland, Gaza as the new Riviera, claim the rights to Ukraine's critical minerals, expunge the facts of history and create alternative facts as it is convenient, frontally attack major universities and research centers for purported antisemitism, sabotage the global economy.

There is a prime example that most vividly reveals the depth of the threat. Putin invaded Ukraine using as a justification a "Mother Russia" interpretation of the region that does not recognize Ukraine as an independent nation-state. Trump raised the ante: Ukraine started the war with Russia, Trump has asserted, and Republicans who previously competed with each other in their opposition to Putin and Russia, either have lost their tongues or wagged them in their approval. This is a remarkable echo of Hannah Arendt's warnings about the dangerous totalitarian relationship between truth and power, as I have already noted in chapter 4, but I return to the example here, risking repetition, to underscore the close fit between Trump's actions and her primary example of totalitarian culture.

Arendt argued that for a sound politics to exist and flourish, philosophical truth should not substitute for political opinions, and that factual truth should be the ground upon which politics operates. Her prime illustrative example: when it comes to the cause of World War I, there will and should be multiple interpretations, but all of them must start with the basic fact that Germany invaded Belgium and not the other way around. Putin and Trump demonstrate the deep challenge we are now facing, confirming her judgment. First, the president of Russia asserts the singular truth of his interpretation of Russian-Ukrainian relationships through an act of war, and then the president of the United States makes sound politics impossible when he declares that it was a war that Ukraine started, in effect declaring that Ukraine invaded Russia, contrary to the factual truth.[46]

It is tempting to conclude that we are experiencing the end of the "age of democracy," but the uncertainty examined in chapter 2 suggests that this is not necessarily our destiny.

10. Confronting the Enemy: Hope Against Hopelessness

I am not optimistic, but I know I should resist overly deterministic pessimism. Doing so, I must qualify the argument of the preceding chapters. I concede a certain one-sidedness of our inquiry. In the chapters, I have focused on the overlooked: the beauty of the gray and the radical importance of the center. I have critically highlighted the importance of complexity and ambiguity, and the promise of public deliberations and commitment to compromise. I downplayed the obvious: compromise has its limits, and sometimes those with whom we disagree are enemies, not just opponents. Sometimes it is a black and white matter. Sometimes the goal must be to vanquish an enemy, not to come to a mutually acceptable, less than ideal agreement. While the enemy, as I see it, has been implicit through much of our inquiry, it became more apparent in chapter 9. In conclusion, I want to make it explicit, identifying what I take to be today's primary enemy, considering ways of responding from the radical center, defending the center, and then illuminating grounds for hope of turning back the retreat of democracy.

The Enemy: The Neo-Totalitarians

From the point of view of our inquiry, those who would destroy a free public life must be defeated, even as there isn't one single road to victory. In identifying this enemy, I am following the lead of Hannah Arendt in her account in *The Origins of Totalitarianism*. In my reading, hers is a study of the destruction of the public, of the substitution of philosophy for political action among the Greeks, of the rejection of the world for the kingdom of heaven in Christendom, and the confusion between public and private with the ascendance of the court and society in the modern age, and mass society in her times. "Antisemitism," "Imperialism," and "Totalitarianism," the three parts of her book, are, in her understanding, developments within this world-rejecting, receding of public life tradition. In chapter 4, I show how I came to this reading. Here I emphasize the political implications. I want to recognize this primary insight about the totalitarianism of her times and apply it to our times. The totalitarian project is the project of destroying a free public space, and we are now observing a new manifestation of the project. It should both be clearly identified and then opposed with a gray sensibility and a fundamental commitment to defending this space.

Consider an example reported in chapter 8: Adam Michnik demonstrated these two points in his writing and public engagement. In his *The Church and the Left*, he argued that developments in the Catholic Church and among secular left-wing intellectuals opened an opportunity for them to oppose Communist domination, and then collaborate, despite their differences. A line was drawn for a struggle, not to convince the ruling power, but to replace it. Yet, within this field of contestation, Michnik in "The New Evolutionism," recognized that there were different ways of struggling against the powers, including those who had fought against the regime through some collaboration with it. Crucially, his new evolutionism among multiple political and social currents is pitted against a common enemy, the totalitarian regime. He called for collaboration among opponents against the enemy, the regime.

We find ourselves in a circumstance that has important similarities but also important differences. It is alike in that the autocratic regimes of our times are analogously constituted through the ironic relationship between true belief and cynicism. It is different because ours is a time when the inertia of events, their evolution, is pointing in an anti-democratic direction.

The task is to change the direction.

It has become imperative to understand who the enemy is and to avoid playing, intentionally or unintentionally, into its hands. While the enemy comes in many guises, it has a common feature: it attacks free public life. It works to limit and control critical media. It undermines the independence of institutions of higher education and research. It rallies its supporters against demonized segments of the population, i.e., all its perceived enemies: the foreign-born, immigrants, independent women, racial and sexual minorities, the urban, and the elites, among others.

Our enemies in the United States, and far beyond, transgress democratic norms and practices, as they identify their partisan position and the personality of their leader, with the common good and the interests of the nation, and they confuse public service with their private gain. In the technical language of sociological theory, they de-differentiate the institutions of modern society.[47] In the imagination of today's authoritarians, everything is subject to the leaders' and their vassals' political judgment and will. The independent logics of the economy, law, the arts and sciences, and even religion are stifled. Such was a notable, fundamental feature of totalitarians of the twentieth century, and again it is characteristic of the "neo-totalitarians" of the twenty-first. It is archetypically evident in the imagination and practice of Donald Trump and his collaborators.

The Response

With the enemy identified, the position of a radical centrist takes priority. Where possible, direct political opposition is called for, to decisively defeat the neo-totalitarians. Worldwide, democrats of the left, right, and center, political opponents on many issues, have been collaborating toward this end. While this is the most forthright way to turn back the anti-democratic wave, there are challenges concerning the grounds for collaboration and its timing.

In the United States, for example, Democrats, Republicans, and independents[48] must act in mutually supportive ways. There are two related but not identical goals: to defeat Donald Trump and his supporters in every electoral context where this is possible, and to turn back the retreat of democracy in America, to get to the point that not every election is between two parties, one that supports democracy in America, the other that systematically undermines it. There is, thus, simultaneously a need to collaborate across the democratic political spectrum and the need to create a new party system, in which political opponents can confront each other based on competing interests and principles. Collaborating across the political spectrum will involve uniting to support candidates against the Republican Party, supporting either independents, of one sort or another, or Democratic Party candidates. Changing the political system means there is also a need for an alternative to the Democratic Party to emerge, worthy opponents who democratically compete, a revived Republican Party, a new dominant second party to the right, or the left of the Democrats. These two goals are in tension. When should opponents join forces? When should they compete? When should those who seek a return to the liberal-democratic status quo ante work with those who seek a progressive transformation of that form of democracy? When should they compete with each other?

The struggle is to distinguish opponents from enemies, to work together against the common enemy so that opponents can democratically compete.

This challenge is global, though in most other places it involves party coalitions, which gives them greater flexibility than the two-party system of the United States. Nonetheless, putting together the coalitions that will permanently marginalize neo-totalitarianism should be the major challenge for electoral politics. To say the least, this is difficult, and it sometimes appears to be impossible.

And in more clearly repressive conditions, such as those in Afghanistan, this appearance is even more forbidding. Yet, they still can fight against their repression by creating alternatives for themselves, by working on the details of democracy and strengthening the individuals, groups, and institutions that do this work. This is the lesson I learned in my journey years ago behind the Iron Curtain, considered here in chapters 3 and 8. It is the primary theme of my book, *The Politics of Small Things*. It is the lesson I taught at the American University of Afghanistan. Chapter 6 explored this. I believe this lesson should be applied in the United States and many other established democracies that are now under threat, with a radical appreciation of the centrality of a free public life, and with an appreciation of the beauty of the gray in political affairs.

Hope

Working against despair, I close with reflections on a series of interrelated contestations that illuminate my hope against apparent hopelessness. They combine an appreciate of the beauty of the gray, but also an appreciation of the black and the white, raising the challenge of distinguishing between these two beauties. The examples promise the possibility of some success in intolerable situations and show that limited successes can be achieved.

American Universities: I have long been concerned with the viability of universities in the United States. The public's expectations of colleges and universities have long been at odds with how these institutions have functioned. The key to a most successful academic career has long been a productive research and publishing record, "publish or perish." Teaching excellence has played a secondary role. The public, in contrast, generally only recognizes teaching. And even when it comes to teaching, there is a stark contrast between how those of us who are inside institutions of higher learning view things and how those on the outside do.

We professors generally approach teaching in one of two ways. We seek to impart the knowledge of our disciplined field of study to students, or we try to teach students how our disciplined knowledge can contribute to a general well-rounded education, cultivating informed citizens, capable of critical thinking, as they pursue their public and private lives. As Socrates would have it, we do so because "an unexamined life is not worth living." Some in the broader public may recognize the value of such an education, but for politicians and parents of college students, ultimately, there is a "bottom line." Education is measured by how it enhances vocational prospects, as in, "get a good education to get a good job."

I have long observed with wonder that this disjuncture had not led to a crisis. In the present political environment, the crisis is upon us, supercharged by anti-intellectualism, racism, and "anti-wokeism," as well as a gap between the political consensus in universities and the political consensus in the society beyond universities.

The attacks are clear and present: the purging of DEI programs, mandating and enforcing "intellectual diversity" in courses, programs, and colleges and universities, measuring the cost-benefit ratio of higher educational institutions and programs, and deporting dissident students and professors. Candidates for tenure have been found wanting because state reviews have judged them to be offering courses that do not measure up to intellectual diversity mandates, i.e., they don't include conservative, patriotic thinkers. Dozens, if not hundreds, have been fired because of their DEI work. States have denied First Amendment protections for professors in their classrooms, effectively denying that academic freedom is protected by law. The funding for scientific research has been radically cut. Students protesting injustice as they see it, specifically in protests against the atrocities in Israel, Gaza, and the West Bank, have been arrested, expelled, and deported. And some university administrators are acting to collaborate with outside pressures even before they have been applied, utilizing anticipatory compliance not simply to defend their institutions but also to increase administrative prerogatives to define the academic mission of the university, independent of faculty judgment and self-governance.

The American Association of University Professors has worked against the attacks, as has its competitor organization, the Foundation for Individual Rights and Expression. While these two organizations have profound differences over the support of academic boycotts and issues of DEI, one leaning left, the other leaning right, they have at times stood together against attempts to regulate campus speech and teaching. While some university presidents have been eager to bend to the forces compromising academic freedom, others are steadfastly defending their institutions on their own and collaborating with each other. Presidents Alan

Garber of Harvard, Michael Roth of Wesleyan University, and Christopher Eisgruber of Princeton University have been outstanding.

But most significantly, the repressive forces are being opposed by university professors and their students in their everyday practices. To the degree to which we continue to teach and study in a way that is not shaped by the attacks on the university, we are maintaining academic freedom. As we have observed in chapter 6, if we act as if academic freedom is alive and well, and we are not stopped from acting this way, we constitute the reality of academic freedom. If we don't act this way, if we shy away from principled action, the tide will truly be turned against colleges and universities as we have known them. Then my nightmare will become a reality: the colleges and universities of the post-World War II era, my intellectual home as a student and as a professor, may come to be remembered as a golden age that has come to an end.

It is predictable. The enemy will have its wins. Colleges and universities will be taken over. Purported antisemitism will be used to justify radical cuts in federal funding. (I believe a perverse anti-antisemitism is the new McCarthyism.) Institutions will defend themselves by accommodating unjustified demands. Faculty will offer less controversial classes or rename their classes so that they do not appear to challenge the repressive authorities. Some disciplines, such as gender studies and sociology, and historical and social scientific inquiries that focus on enduring systems of racism, sexism, oppression, and privilege will be repressed in some places, but continue with renewed purpose in others.

Sustaining free academic life, resisting repression, or ignoring potential repression can prevail. It is not too late. This requires refusing to collaborate with a real enemy, but also collaborating with those with whom we have important disagreements, cognizant of the tenuous position of colleges and universities in the greater society. We should also act in a way that understands the primacy of academic freedom over our specific political commitments. We may profoundly disagree on pressing issues of our times, for example on the war in Gaza and the future of Israel-Palestine, but we must meet on university grounds as intellectual opponents freely pursuing scholarly inquiry and debate, as opponents, understanding that outside forces who would stifle such inquiry and debate are the enemy. The (radical centrist) commitment to academic freedom should be the priority.

It is a matter of not only what "they" do, but also about what "we" do.

Civil Rights and the Attack on DEI and Wokeism: Along with purported anti-antisemitism, the attacks on DEI and wokeism are directed at universities, but also at many other institutions: corporations, philanthropic foundations, branches and departments of federal, state, and local governments, the military, entertainment and media institutions, libraries, and primary and secondary schools. In my judgment, these attacks are manifestly racist, and I struggle to understand how it is that so many of my fellow citizens find them acceptable. I suppose it is because the progress that I had imagined Americans had made since my youth was not as deep and as broad as I had thought. Yet perhaps it's also because of the problematic nature of many DEI programs, and the foolishness of many so-called woke actions.

While I think that the ideals of diversity, equity, and inclusion are impossible to oppose on principled democratic grounds, the way they have been operationalized has left much to be desired. Endless instructional videos and forms to be filled out, with bureaucratic professionals administering and reviewing performance measurements. It became a cottage industry.

Likewise, it is also hard to understand how the desire to make the marginalized comfortable, respecting those who have been historically denigrated, and ensuring that language usage is not hurtful, and free speech doesn't silence those who have not traditionally spoken, can be viewed as a problem. Those who are accused of being woke hold these positions. Yet, the way the positions have been instituted have had serious problems: endless examinations and discussions about who can say what, when and how, chastising those who question or are unaware of new norms of deference, and deplatforming speakers that go against the grain of the academic political consensus.

Yet, such criticism has been weaponized for authoritarian purposes. The distance between, on the one hand, the principles behind DEI efforts, and, on the other, their enactment, have made their advocates vulnerable to cynical criticism. Just mentioning the terms diversity, equity, and inclusion has been forbidden under the Trump regime, along with hundreds of other words and phrases, and any attempt to right past wrongs of racial, gender, and sexual discriminations, or even to document the histories of these wrongs.

There have been problems with DEI as it has been practiced and with what is described by its critics as "wokeism." I have wondered whether the monitoring of speech has homogenized discussion. I have been concerned that the valorization of the diversity of identities has limited the range of intellectual perspectives. I am critical of those who would unreflectively apply the ethical and cultural standards of the present in their social circles to those of the past in very different social environments. Criticism of DEI and wokeism has some validity. Yet, I also believe that the attacks on these practices have infinitely more negative consequences than the practices themselves. I am not wishy-washy on this. Quite to the contrary, I think that the best way to resist racist, sexist, homophobic, and transphobic attacks is not to double down on problematic practices, but to interrogate them and develop alternatives through free and open discussion, while forthrightly opposing the attacking powers of the Trump regime.

Free speech: I believe the principled commitment and practice of free speech, broadly understood, is the ultimate grounds for hope against hopelessness in our present moment. Thus, with the previous examples in mind:

1. At universities and in the broader society, there is an urgent need for dialogue. For the democratic political forces of the left, right, and center, to act in concert against the neo-totalitarian threat, they must speak to each other, freely and openly, with mutual respect.

2. To address the problems in Israel-Palestine, and of democracy, diversity, and inclusion, and racism and sexism in the academy, there must be mutually respectful dialogue among the conflicting parties.

3. To fight the authoritarian instrumentalization of the anti-antisemitism attack against universities, a broad and open, mutually respectful, dialogue is again required.

4. As it is also required to turn back racist and sexist attacks upon academic freedom in the university, and upon political freedom there, and in the greater society.

Sustaining free, mutually respectful speech is both a crucial means, and an important end. While it doesn't guarantee that the authoritarian forces around the globe will be overcome, it is a necessary first step, as it increases the chances of victory, and it makes it more likely that the victory will endure. I maintain this fully aware that criticisms of free speech are ubiquitous across the political spectrum, and also with full awareness of how difficult such speech can be to sustain.

There have been subtle but impassioned disagreements about free speech in academic circles and beyond. There is alarm that the academic left is abandoning the ideals of free speech and academic freedom. In contrast, there is also the judgment that free-speech fundamentalists have been using the ideal to ignore the challenges of including the previously marginalized into academic and broader public life, using free speech as a smoke screen for conservative projects. There is further a contested argument that all speech communities are bounded.[49] This controversy is a contemporary variation on an old theme, with important political consequences.

Should we celebrate the freedom of a limited democratic public life such as that which existed in ancient Greece or the early years of the American republic? Or was such freedom so restrictive that it really is its opposite, slave societies, in which the vast majority of the people were excluded from public life? With our understanding of what a democratic society should be, quite different from the ideas and practices of classical Greece and revolutionary America, we understand that if the practice of free speech excludes, it is compromised. But making sure that it doesn't exclude, as the principled advocates of DEI promote, and as the critics of micro-aggressions demonstrate, has led to ideas of speech codes, and excluding those whose practices exclude others. There is an irresolvable dilemma in this, a crucial instance of the social condition. I believe it can't be resolved definitively. It must be resolved publicly, politically. Certainty is the problem. A continual grappling with uncertainty presents an opportunity. Understanding this is a crucial gray basis for hope.

As Michnik called upon the opponents of the Communist regime to talk to each other to oppose their common enemy, I think it is necessary to freely talk to each other against the enemy of our day. Opponents needn't agree, as the secular leftists and the Catholics in Poland surely did not, but we need to act together against our enemy.

Pro-Palestinian and pro-Israeli activists on universities must find the capacity to talk to each other freely so that those who are outside the university and hostile to it don't use the academic conflicts to justify their attacks. Those who are concerned about the attacks on academic freedom from the left and those who are concerned about the limitations on academic freedom and free speech from the right must identify their common enemy in those who are straightforwardly hostile to universities, the life of the mind, the arts, and sciences. Regardless of our political commitments, all academics should support their students and colleagues from elsewhere from politically motivated arrests and deportations.

Final Note

These chapters and the lectures upon which they have been based were originally composed for presentation in different places and at different times in the relatively recent past. I've been writing the book, in turn, in the eye of a storm, with an evident worldwide retreat from democracy, with the United States, the most powerful country in the world, leading the charge, with a brutal war raging in a small but symbolically significant corner of the world, and with the reordering of the geopolitical and economic order. I have been unsure about how to close the inquiry since the retreat and the struggle against it are ongoing. I've been arguing against the temptation of projecting the anti-democratic trend into the future. I've been arguing against despair. I've been trying to explain why such projection is a mistake. Yet, it's also a mistake to believe that this trend will naturally be turned back, that we are at the downside of the cycle and that things will naturally improve.

We are between past and future. What we do will determine what happens next. We may or may not be able to sustain a coalition of democrats against the looming threat of authoritarianism around the world. But even if we can't, we may be able to resist the trend in one or more social settings: perhaps at universities, or in news and media institutions, or libraries, or localities—villages, towns, cities, states, or regions. Perhaps one country or collection of countries will take the lead, perhaps with the United States, perhaps against the United States. It is my conviction, argued from various angles in this book, that the major trend of democracies retreating can be turned back if we appreciate that gray is beautiful and if we commit ourselves to free public life, as a primary, radical priority.

The neo-totalitarians present multiple challenges that can and should be opposed. With an appreciation of the beauty of the gray and the importance of the radical center, they can be opposed systematically by national and international political coalitions. They can and should also be opposed more precisely in defense of crucial democratic principles: the rule of law, freedom of speech and protest, freedom of assembly, and in defense of essential democratic institutions: schools, colleges, universities and research institutions, libraries, museums, and the press, publishing, and other news and information media. I am not optimistic, but action does provide grounds for hope.

Notes

1   I have found Phillip Sands's investigation of the origins of the concepts of "crimes against humanity" and "genocide" very helpful in coming to the judgment of the Gaza genocide. I found especially cogent his reflections on the necessity of applying the concept despite the pitfalls of using it.

2   Michnik, "Gray is Beautiful," 15.

3   Michnik, "Gray is Beautiful," 18.

4   Michnik, "Gray is Beautiful," 18.

5   For a number of years, every Friday, I published a "Gray Friday" essay on *Public Seminar* and continued publishing these essays on the publishing platform of *Democracy Seminar*. For a sample of these essays see: https://publicseminar. org/?s=Gray+Fridays and https://democracyseminar.newschool.org/author/ jgoldfarb/.

6   Analysts who map out what I am calling the radical centrist position on Israel-Palestine are Rashid Khalidi and David Grossman, an anti-Zionist and a Zionist who pay attention to the opinions and judgments of their opponents.

7   Described in chapter 3.

8   Analyzed systematically in chapter 8.

9   As we will observe below, these principles and practices are now under attack, and the result is only uncertain. I am not an optimist, though I do have my grounds for hope, which I will explore as we proceed.

10 Analyzed in greater detail in Chapter 8.

11 *Rolling Transition and the Role of Intellectuals*, 2023.

12 Analyzed in detail in the concluding chapters.

13 I note here the parallel to the Israeli-Hamas conflict in Gaza. See the conclusion in which I develop this.

14 This is analyzed in chapter 10.

15 See the work of *Deliberately Considered* at https://www.deliberatelyconsidered. com/.

16 Explored in detail in chapter 6.

17 Arendt, *Men in Dark Times*, viii.

18 Arendt, *Men in Dark Times*, ix

19 Here I am exploring the post 9/11 experience. For an application of the same insight to the global situation in 2025, see chapter 9.

20 Arendt, *Men in Dark Times*, viii.

21 This is developed in chapter 8.

22 How this works in our world is analyzed in chapter 9.

23 Hannah Arendt "What is Freedom?," in *Between Past and Future*, 154–55.

24 This is how she concludes *The Origins*. It is highlighted in her chapter "Ideology and Terror." The implications of this analysis to our times are explored in chapter 10.

25 I actually have reservations about this common observation, because I believe that the term ideology has more specific meaning than such an assertion assumes. I address this issue in *Civility and Subversion*.

26 A selection of her writings of this time can be found in her *The Jew as Pariah*.

27 Arendt, *The Jew as Pariah*, 186.

28 See Omri Boehm, *The Haifa Republic* for a provocative examination of this potential.

29 This section of the lecture was drawn from an analysis that first appeared in *The Cynical Society*.

30 Crouch, "Aunt Medea." 41-42.

31 Note here the creative role uncertainty plays in Morrison's work. This confirms the analysis in chapter 2.

32 I directed an extension of my AUAF teaching, "Civic Engagement in Repressive Contexts," for the Open Society University Network with students from Asia, Africa, Europe, and the Americas.

33 This opening of the course builds upon the findings of my first two books, *The Persistence of Freedom* and *On Cultural Freedom*.

34 More on the challenges of collaboration in chapter 9 below.

35 These quotes are taken from a draft of her dissertation that Dastageer shared with me, in Dastageer, "Between Two Fires: Narrating Non-Agency in the Afghan Peace Talks."

36 At regular intervals, the AUAF security officer in Kabul sends out messages concerning continued terrorist attacks, natural disasters, and political developments from around the country.

37 Two of the other papers presented to the conference were on Douglas and Wells, See *Public Seminar* https://publicseminar.org/issues/2023-02-02/.

38 This is developed more fully in the concluding chapters.

39 This is now most evident in the workings of the electoral college, which often leads to the election of a candidate who failed to receive the majority of the vote.

40 Tocqueville, *Democracy in America*, 403.

41 See Phillip Bump, "Donald Trump's Father was arrested after a Klan riot in Queens," *Washington Post*, https://www.washingtonpost.com/news/the-fix/wp/2016/02/28/in-1927-donald-trumps-father-was-arrested-after-a-klan-riot-in-queens/, Wayne Madsen, "The America of Trump's Father," *Scoop*, October 8, 2019, https://www.scoop.co.nz/stories/HL1910/S00036/the-america-of-trumps-father.htm, and Krishnadev Calamur, "A Short History of 'America First,'" *The Atlantic*, January 21, 2017, https://www.theatlantic.com/politics/archive/2017/01/trump-america-first/514037/.

42 Michnik, "The New Evolutionism," in *Letters from Prison and Other Essays*, 145.

43 Havel, *The Power of the Powerless*, 6.

44 Havel, *The Power of the Powerless*, 14–15.

45 Havel, *The Power of the Powerless*, 18.

46 As this book goes to press, Trump reversed himself, with little explanation. He wanted to heroically end the war. Putin insisted on pursuing it to realize his ultra-nationalist aims. Trump realized that what he perceived as his warm personal relationship with Putin didn't yield the result he imagined. Trump expressed his deep disappointment and increased military support for Ukraine. The MAGA crowd, for the most part, supported this turn of events. This reminded me of Stalin's changes in policy surrounding the Molotov-Ribbentrop Pact at the beginning of World War II.

47 I analyze how this works in *Beyond Glasnost*.

48 Independents are, in fact, the majority of the population that includes the highly active who are engaged in politics outside the highly institutionalized two-party system, and the less active, who are simply not affiliated. One major school of thought suggests that moving the latter group is key in deciding closely contested elections.

49 Stanley Fish has directly addressed this issue in his work.

References

Adorno, Theodor. *Prisms*. MIT Press, 1982.

Arendt, Hannah. *Between Past and Future*. Penguin Books, 1977.

Arendt, Hannah. *Eichmann in Jerusalem: A Report on the Banality of Evil*. Penguin Books, 1965.

Arendt, Hannah. *The Human Condition*. University of Chicago Press, 1958.

Arendt, Hannah. *The Jew as Pariah*. Grove Press, 1978.

Arendt, Hannah. *Men in Dark Times*. Harcourt, Brace & World, 1968.

Arendt, Hannah. *On Revolution*. Viking Press, 1965.

Arendt, Hannah. *The Origins of Totalitarianism*. Harcourt, Brace, Jovanovich, 1957.

Bellah, Robert N., Richard Madsen, William M. Sullivan, Ann Swidler, and Steven M. Tipton. *Habits of the Heart*. University of California Press, 1985.

Boehm, Omri. *The Haifa Republic*. New York Review Books, 2022.

Bozóki, András. *Rolling Transition and the Role of Intellectuals*. Central European University Press, 2023.

Crouch, Stanley. "Aunt Medea," review of *Beloved* by Toni Morrison. *New Republic*, October 19, 1987, 38–43.

Dastageer, Muska. "Between Two Fires: Narrating Non-Agency in the Afghan Peace Talks." PhD diss., University of Sydney, forthcoming.

Dekel, Irit. *Mediation at the Holocaust Memorial in Berlin*. Palgrave Macmillan, 2013.

Durkheim, Emile, *The Division of Labor in Society*, Pelgrave, 1984.

Eliasoph, Nina. *The Politics of Volunteering*. Polity, 2013.

Fish, Stanley. *There's No Such Thing As Free Speech: And It's a Good Thing, Too*. Oxford University Press, 1993.

Foucault, Michel. *The Foucault Reader*. Edited by Paul Rabinow. Pantheon Books, 1984.

Foucault, Michel. "Truth and Power." In *The Foucault Reader*, edited by Paul Rabinow. Pantheon Books, 1984.

Fraser, Nancy. *Cannibal Capitalism*. Verso, 2023.

Friedman, Milton, *Capitalism and* Freedom, University of Chicago Press, 1962

Garfinkel, Harold. *Studies in Ethnomethodology*. Polity, 1991.

Geertz, Clifford. *The Interpretation of Cultures*. Basic Books, 2017.

Gessen, Masha. *Surviving Autocracy*. Penguin, 2021.

Gilger, Patrick. *The Subject of Public Religion: How Religious Practices Build Democratic Citizens,* University of Notre Dame Press, forthcoming.

Goffman, Erving. *Interaction Ritual: Essays in Face to Face Behavior*. Pantheon, 1982.

Goffman, Erving. *The Presentation of Self in Everyday Life*. Anchor, 1959.

Goldfarb, Jeffrey C. *After the Fall: The Pursuit of Democracy in Central Europe*. Basic Books, 1992.

Goldfarb, Jeffrey C. *Beyond Glasnost: The Post-Totalitarian Mind*. University of Chicago Press, 1989.

Goldfarb, Jeffrey C. *Civility and Subversion: The Intellectual in Democratic Society*. Cambridge University Press, 1998.

Goldfarb, Jeffrey C. *The Cynical Society: The Culture of Politics and the Politics of Culture in American Life*. University of Chicago Press, 1991.

Goldfarb, Jeffrey C. *On Cultural Freedom: An Exploration of Public Life in Poland and America*. University of Chicago Press, 1983.

Goldfarb, Jeffrey C. *The Persistence of Freedom: The Sociological Implications of Polish Student Theater*. Westview, 1980.

Goldfarb, Jeffrey C. *The Politics of Small Things: The Power of the Powerless in Dark Times*. University of Chicago Press, 2006.

Goldfarb, Jeffrey C. *Reinventing Political Culture: The Power of Culture versus the Culture of Power*. Polity Press, 2011.

Goldfarb, Jeffrey C. "Social Bases of Independent Public Expression in Communist Societies." *American Journal of Sociology* 83, no. 4 (January 1978): 920–39.

Goldfarb, Jeffrey C. "Teaching the Classics: Reflections of an ex-Marxist Wannabe." *Deliberately Considered*, September 20, 2011. https://www.deliberatelyconsidered.com/2011/09/teaching-the-classics-reflections-of-an-ex-marxist-wannabe/index.html.

Goldfarb, Jeffrey C. "What Do You Mean When You Use the Term Neo-Liberalism?" *Public Seminar*, April 7, 2017. https://publicseminar.org/2017/04/what-do-you-mean-when-you-use-the-term-neoliberalism/.

Grossman, David. *The Thinking Heart*. Vintage, 2025.

Gutman, Yifat. *Memory Activism*. Vanderbilt University Press, 2017.

Haekkerup, Nick, and William Milberg. "The American Dream Comes to Life in Denmark." *Public Seminar*, October 22, 2013. https://publicseminar.org/2013/10/the-american-dream-comes-to-life-in-denmark/.

Habermas, Jürgen, *The Structural Transformation of the Public Sphere*, M.I.T. Press, 1991.

Hanrahan, Nancy. *Differences in Time*. Praeger, 2000.

Havel, Vaclav. *The Power of the Powerless*. Vintage Classics, 2018.

Hollander, Paul. *Political Pilgrims*. Routledge, 1997.

Horkheimer, Max and Theodore Adorno, *The Dialectic of Enlightenment*, Stanford University Press, 2007.

Isaac, Jeffrey C. *#Against Trump: Notes from Year One*. OR Books, 2018.

Jacoby, Russel. *The Last Intellectuals*. Basic Books, 2000.

Janowitz, Morris. *The Professional Soldier*. Free Press, 2017.

Johnson, Paul. *Intellectuals*. Harper Perennial, 2007.

Jonas, Hans. "The Burdens and Blessings of Mortality." *Hastings Center Report* 22, no. 1 (1992): 34–40. https://doi.org/10.2307/3562722.

Khalidi, Rashid. *The Hundred Years War on Palestine*. Metropolitan Books, 2021.

Kuron, Jacek and Karol Modzelewski, "Open Letter to the Party." Published in translation as *Revolutionary Marxist Students in Poland Speak Out*, Merit Publishers, 1968.

Latour, Bruno. *Reassembling the Social: An Introduction to Actor-Network-Theory*. Oxford University Press, 2007.

Levine, Donald. *The Flight from Ambiguity*. University of Chicago Press, 1988.

Levisky, Steven, and Daniel Ziblatt. *How Democracies Die*. Crown, 2019.

Lin, Maya. "Making of the Memorial." *The New York Review*, November 2, 2000. https://www.nybooks.com/articles/2000/11/02/making-the-memorial/.

Linz, Juan J., and Alfred Stepan. *Problems of Democratic Transition and Consolidation*. Johns Hopkins University Press, 1996.

Lipski, Jan Jósef. *KOR: A History of the Workers Defense Committee in Poland, 1976-1981*. University of California Press, 1985.

Marcuse, Herbert. "The Critique of Repressive Tolerance." In *A Critique of Pure Tolerance*, edited by Robert Paul Wolff, Barrington Moore Jr., and Herbert Marcuse, 81–117. Beacon Press 1965.

Matynia, Elżbieta. *Performative Democracy*. Routledge, 2015.

Merton, Robert. *Sociological Ambivalence and Other Essays*. Free Press, 1976.

Metz, Zachary. "The Intimacy of Enemies: Peacebuilding and the Politics of Small Things." *European Journal of Cultural and Political Sociology* 11, no. 3 (2024): 366–78.

Michels, Robert. *Political Parties: A Sociological Study of the Oligarchical Tendencies of Modern Democracy*. Free Press, 1966.

Michnik, Adam. "Gray is Beautiful: Thoughts on Democracy in Central Europe." *Dissent* 44 (Spring 1997): 14.

Michnik, Adam. *The Church and the Left*. University of Chicago Press, 1993.

Michnik, Adam. *Letters from Prison and Other Essays*. University of California Press, 1987.

Milosz, Czeslaw. *Captive Mind*. Vintage, 1990.

Moore Jr., Barrington. *Social Origins of Dictatorship and Democracy*. Beacon Press, 1966.

Moore Jr., Barrington. *Injustice*. Palgrave Macmillan, 1978.

Murray, Albert. *The Omni-Americans*. Library of Congress, 2020.

Nisbet, Robert. *The Twilight of Authority*. Liberty Fund, 2000.

Olick, Jeffrey. *The Sins of the Fathers: Germany, Memory, Method*. University of Chicago Press, 2016.

Parsons, Talcott. *The System of Modern Societies*. Prentice Hall, 1971.

Putnam, Robert. *Bowling Alone*. Simon and Schuster, 2020.

Rorty, Richard. *Contingency, Irony and Solidarity*. Cambridge University Press, 1989.

Said, Edward. *Representations of the Intellectual*. Vintage, 1996.

Sands, Philippe, *East West: The Origins of "Genocide" and Crimes "Against Humanity*," Knopf, 2017.

Sennett, Richard. *The Fall of Public Man*. W. W. Norton, 1992.

Simmel, Georg. *Georg Simmel on Individuality and Social Forms*. Edited by Donald Levine. University of Chicago Press, 1972.

Snyder, Timothy. *On Tyranny*. Crown, 2017.

Tarde, Gabrielle. *Gabrielle Tarde on Communication and Social Influence*. University of Chicago Press, 2011.

Thomas W. I., and Dorothy Swain Thomas. *The Child in America*. Alfred A. Knopf, 1928.

de Tocqueville, Alexis. *Democracy in America*. University of Chicago Press, 2002.

Wagner Pacifici, Robin. *Theorizing the Standoff: Contingency in Action.* Cambridge University Press, 2000.

Wagner, Izabela. *Bauman: A Biography.* Polity, 2020.

Weber, Max. "Politics as a Vocation." In *From Max Weber: Essays in Sociology,* edited and translated by H. H. Gerth and C. Wright Mills, 77–128. Oxford University Press, 1946.

Index of Names

Index of Subjects

minority rights, 20, 21
modern liberal democracy, 62–63, 129

National Mall, 81–82
National Socialist, 161
NATO *see* North Atlantic Treaty
    Organization
Nazis, 57, 75, 80, 110, 125, 129
neo-totalitarianism, 169–71, 172,
    173, 179, 182
"The New Evolutionism" (Michnik),
    41, 108, 129, 132–35, 152–53,
    170
new leftist, 17, 29, 30, 31, 32–35
New Left Organizing Committee, 32,
    34, 40
New School for Social Research, 1,
    34, 37, 41–42, 43, 55–56, 89–90
9/11 attacks, 47–49, 59
North Atlantic Treaty Organization
    (NATO), 144, 151
Notes on the State of Virginia
    (Jefferson), 114

October 7, 2023, Hamas attack,
    4–6, 72
official truth, 63, 67, 149, 162
On Cultural Freedom (Goldfarb),
    95, 101–2
On Revolution (Arendt), 56
opposition, 2, 42, 44, 45, 48, 58–59,
    110, 135–36, 142
oppression, 3, 33, 60, 104, 176
The Origins of Totalitarianism
    (Arendt), 43, 56, 58–59, 63,
    65–66, 161, 169–70

Palestinian Jews, 75
Palestinians, 74, 75, 93
    domination of, 94
    Gaza, 4–6, 72, 127, 159, 166,
        175, 177

Israeli conflict with, 4–6, 70–73,
    179
pro-, 5, 49, 73, 181
the Party, 66, 107
    Communist, 37, 39, 63, 132–35,
        139, 141, 148, 161–62
    confliction in, 5–6, 179
    Democratic, 48, 126, 128, 143,
        172
    Independent, 172
    Republican, 126, 127, 128,
        147–48, 172
    role of, 22
passive collaborator, 134, 135, 136,
    137, 140, 141, 142
PAX (progressive Catholic organiza-
    tion), 130, 140
the Pentagon, 47
Peoples Republic of Poland, 35, 129
philosophical truth, 62–63, 167
pluralism, 21, 117, 119
Poland
    Auschwitz, 75, 76, 88
    Catholicism in, 130, 133, 140,
        181
    Kaczynski, 7, 86
    political landscapes in, 57
    post-war, 130, 140
    Solidarność in, 36, 39–41, 47–48,
        58, 69, 96, 107, 133–36, 140
    Soviet bloc, 2, 19, 29, 31, 46, 61,
        63, 67, 96, 107, 111, 133
    Warsaw, 1, 3, 36–37, 41–43, 59,
        131–32
Polish Student Theater, 26, 36–39,
    41, 48
political actors, 13, 75, 94
political alliances, 62
political approach, 37
political collaboration, 51, 90, 128
political commitment, 146, 148, 177,
    181

For Product Safety Concerns and Information please contact our EU
representative GPSR@taylorandfrancis.com
Taylor & Francis Verlag GmbH, Kaufingerstraße 24, 80331 München, Germany